AWAKENING

Rev. Dr. Norma Edwards

ISBN 978-1-955156-56-1 (paperback)
ISBN 978-1-955156-57-8 (digital)

Rushmore Press LLC
1 800 460 9188
www.rushmorepress.com

Printed in the United States of America

TO MY CHILDREN
Marcus
Andrew
Hazel
Michelle
Stephen
Thank you for the love and much gratitude for the support.

Be
Like a page that aches for a word
Which speaks to a theme
That is timeless
Sing
As a song in search of a voice
That is silent
And the one God will make for your day
—Neil Diamond

ACKNOWLEDGMENTS

This labor of love has been supported by the collaboration of so many beautiful souls whose names are far too many to mention here.

First, I acknowledge my beloved husband, Calvin, who has been my compass and inspiration throughout the writing process. Thank you to my amazing family (nuclear and extended) for your ever-loving presence and support in my life.

To my literary agent, Richard Shaw of Rushmore Press, you instantly recognized the value of my work and put a dedicated team to work to make the dream a reality. There were so many people who contributed time, energy, instruction, and guidance throughout my spiritual journey. The wisdom keepers, past and present; the teachers, young and old alike; way-showers who fell in step to support the energy; earth angels and the "inner circle"— you know who you are—thank you for you kept the light burning brightly along the way.

To the clinicians I have had the privilege to work alongside, you opened the door and let me in, and I will always be grateful. A special "thank you" to the men and women residents on cell-blocks in prisons and residents at the re-entry center in Washington, D.C where I provided Chaplain and therapeutic services. Thank you for allowing me to be of service. You bared your souls; we journeyed through to redemption.

My greatest blessing has been the opportunities afforded to me to be of service on the planet. It was certainly a two-way street—we learned from each other as we journeyed along the way. Together, we caught a glimpse of God's amazing grace in action in your lives and mine. The results of the journey have lit an eternal spark of hope within my heart—I leave you my readers with a nugget of wisdom.

*"Remember to entertain strangers for thereby
some have entertained angels along the way."*

CHAPTER ONE

You could well say that the drama of my life began well before my birth into this world. My teenage mother, in defiance of her parents, fell in love with a married man much older than herself. She became pregnant which caused not only a crisis in a prominent family but also shook the very structure of the church. Both of my parents sang in the local community church choir and as church people would say "they took to each other like wildfire" while rehearsing *The Messiah* for the Easter Sunday service. This "sinful and scandalous act" as it was labeled by church folk caused an uproar not only in the church but also in the community in which they lived. My soon-to-be-parents became the gossip and talk of the town. In a culture where tradition not just expected but dictated that "well brought up" young ladies should be virgins at the time of marriage, this was indeed a grave violation of tradition as well as church doctrine. To the backdrop of all of this, the church as well as the community awaited with bated breath the sitting pastor's decision and the action he would take since the scandal involved one of his daughters. My grandfather, the pastor of the local Brethren Church, was a man of God with very strong religious convictions. He followed the doctrine of the church, stood up in the pulpit one Sunday morning, and read his daughter and my soon-to-be father out of the church. My grandmother, on hearing the news, said she'd rather die than face the shame. She took to her bed, had a heart attack, and died soon after the announcement was made. My pregnant mother sat in her pew shamed and scared, experiencing total disconnection at a time when she most needed support. Being "readout" of the church really meant out of her family as well and also shunned by the community.

My aunt, one of her three sisters in a prominent and God-fearing family, bravely stood up that Sunday morning and made an announcement. She and her new husband would take my mother and the baby into their humble home. For this action on their part, they too were promptly readout of the church. According to the church, their guilt was that they were about to harbor sin in their home. My mother was made by her sister to swear to have nothing to do with my soon-to-be father. It was a promise she kept for twelve long years of her life. The tradition in which I was raised taught me to firmly believe that babies in the womb do hear and relate to every word spoken on the outside. As a baby in the womb, I too was rejected and became a "survivor" of so-called sin and shame.

I entered the world on a rainy day in the middle of the tropical rainy season. My aunt who was at my mother's side said it took hours of labor that culminated in a very difficult delivery. I came out of the womb with a "caul" (a white membrane) covering my face. This was hastily removed by the sympathetic midwife to allow me to take my first breath. The midwife, a wise compassionate, elderly woman, wrapped the membrane in a handkerchief and gently gave it to my mother for safekeeping. She told my mother that the "caul" was considered by the elders to be "sacred" and should be treated as such. My mother was given instructions not to share the information or talk about its existence. However, as it is in third world countries, once the midwife left the hospital, the news had somehow spread throughout the town. My mother's instruction included keeping the "caul" in a safe place until I was old enough for it to be passed to me for safekeeping either when I entered my transition from childhood into adulthood or on the day of my marriage. The elders in our community believed that the presence of the "caul" at birth was a sign that the incoming child entered into the world with a special purpose and with the ability to see into the spiritual as well as the physical worlds. Later in life, my mother described to me how afraid and inadequate she felt when this information was given to her.

My birthplace was Georgetown, the capital of the then British Guiana, a colony owned and colonized by the British at that time. When our independence was acquired from the British, the country was renamed Guyana. It is the only English speaking nation on the

South American Coast—a land situated between mountains and sea with an abundance of natural resources. Some say it's a land made rich by the sunshine and lush by the rains with its only two seasons—hot weather followed by the stormy, rainy season. There is a long history of the activities of the slave trade that brought African people into the country by way of the Middle Passage. At the abolition of slavery, indentured labor (one step above slavery) was introduced. Laborers were recruited from East India from where they left the poverty of their country to seek better lives. British Guiana, as it was during colonial days, was a relatively small country known as "the land of many waters" with a population of less than a million people. The British mined and shipped the vast natural resources of the country for their own benefit leaving the former slaves and the natives in poverty. As it is the customs in small tight-knit communities, every one knows and speaks the history from one generation to another. Interestingly enough, local history more often than not has been found to include a bit of everything, including facts, figures, gossip, and anything else that the locals might find interesting and/or entertaining.

Since my father was a teacher, he was considered to be educated and therefore, a community leader. People looked up to him for guidance and leadership even though they gossiped about the circumstances of my birth. I was constantly reminded by the elders that I had, for example, opened my mother's womb (It was considered more blessed for the womb of a young girl to be opened by a male child); that it rained tumultuously on the day of my birth and for eight days and nine nights thereafter. Towns and villages were flooded, crops and animals lost, and the people in the farming communities suffered greatly because of the rise of water levels. The elders voiced their beliefs that the heavens opened up to usher a "seer" into their midst. There always seemed to be a great deal of speculation about the many signs surrounding my birth. It was clear that because the elders had so many things to say, it gave the locals much to talk about. No one knew for sure whether these signs were good, bad, a freak of nature, or just plain coincidence.

My father, on the other hand, being very spiritual, and despite the restrictive circumstance of my birth, stood his ground and claimed his right according to local custom to name me. My parents were not allowed to communicate with one another at the time of my birth so my father quickly showed up at the registrar's office and named me Norma (interpreted as "the teacher"). Much later in my life, my mother shared with me her agony and how inadequate and unworthy she felt at sixteen years of age—in her own words "branded by the guilt of sin." She was expected to raise what the elders termed as a "gifted" child without support from the "wisdom keepers," the church, or the community. As a grown woman, I showed a keen interest in understanding the differences between the terms "ancestry" and "heritage." I am so thankful for the ancestors who left us with traditions that helped me to appreciate the unique difference between the two. All of this information I discovered was so carefully passed down from generation to generation by way of the oral tradition. Because of this, I've come to recognize that despite the circumstances of my birth, from my father I drew great strength, intellect, and deep spiritual insight; from my mother I received love, nurturing compassion, and unwavering faith in the power of Almighty God. The strength from both sides provided me with persistence and a strong drive to make life work despite all the odds. My mother was a patient listener. Some of my most vivid memories of her were from observing experiences that showed her forgiving nature. This virtue of forgiveness was always evident in her interaction with people from all walks of life. Her interest in giving her talent to the Brethren Church from which she was cast out was a living example of forgiveness. She was a naturally gifted soprano, and the fact that she was not allowed to even enter into her former church building did not stop her from giving her talent there. She privately mentored the church's soprano singer each year to ensure the best quality of sound for their Easter services which she could not attend.

You may well say that I was blessed to be raised in a loving environment by two females—my Aunt Ette as she was called by all the children in the neighborhood and my mother with a heart of gold as my aunt—a sweet, beautiful woman inside and out. Aunt Ette was supported by her husband, a quiet, simple man, fondly referred to as Uncle James in the community. He understood his role as a provider of the family that included me and my mother. As a seaman, he loved the sea and captained a boat that ferried food supplies to and from the Caribbean islands. This work took him away from home for weeks at a time. At home, he kept and maintained a bird sanctuary which included two colorful talking parrots. These two birds provided many hours of lively entertainment for the household as well as the neighbors. We all had to be careful about what we said aloud while around the birds. They were known to repeat catchy phrases from our conversation as well as the "rude" lines from popular calypsoes. The things they choose to repeat were often very hilarious. While Uncle James was away at sea, I enjoyed rising early in the morning to help my aunt take care of the birds. His other love was two Doberman dogs, one of which he took with him to sea while the other remained at home as a watch dog and protector of the family. At sea, he was known to keep a sober head. At home, in his time away from the sea, he enjoyed drinking alone and the bar was the first thing to be stocked when he got home. Often, with a little too much to drink, he became talkative, sang pirate songs, and could sometimes become embarrassingly rowdy. In his sober moments, particularly when he tended to his birds, he would tell us children scary pirate stories and describe for us the beauty of the coral reefs around the islands, in particular his favorite, Jamaica. Later in my life, fascinated by all that I heard about Jamaica, I was left with a yearning for travel to learn about other cultures around the world. I've taken several trips to the Caribbean islands including Jamaica to enjoy the beauty, culture, and easygoing nature of its inhabitants.

Aunt Ette, his wife, was truly her own person and in so many ways, very different from Millie my mother. She was a strikingly beautiful, strong black woman. She had pretty eyes and "good" hair as they say in the black community. She was, so to speak, "a force to be reckoned with." To me, Aunt Ette was my mother's protector. She was the practical voice in the family who wasted no time speaking up, saying things the way she saw/felt them, and would often remind people young or old to "mind their own business." My mother, on the other hand, was shy and beautiful but with the soul of a peacemaker who would go out of her way to avoid conflict at all costs. One of her favorite sayings is:

"Let sleeping dogs lie."

"But Mommie," I would say.

"The maga dog could still rise up to bite you."

"Then we deal with that when it raises its ugly head," I would respond.

That warning still surfaces in my mind and my spirit when I find myself confronted with treachery and discord. She was to me an amateur diplomat who was well endowed with many natural talents.

One of my mother's many talents was singing—her soprano voice blessed the lives of many in the family as well as the community. Her sewing skills kept my aunt in the height of fashion. The two sisters adored each other that even at an early age, I could see that my mother lived comfortably in the shadow of her older sister and liked it that way. Aunt Ette was outgoing; many in the community acknowledged that she possessed healing hands that soothed all the hurts and bruises of the children in the neighborhood. You could say that she was also the equivalent of the native "medicine" woman with an amazing understanding of the healing powers and efficacy of herbs. She and I would sometimes spend an entire afternoon up on the hillside gathering herbs from which she made very effective home-made cough syrup. Neighbors and strangers alike would come to the house to seek herbal remedies to control diabetes, high blood pressure, coughs, and cold. These services were provided free of charge to all who needed them. I would hear my aunt encourage people who came to her for herbal remedies that they also needed to consult a medical doctor when the symptoms were grave. My mother's strengths included being humble, respectful, and ever mindful of her listening role in any given situation. She liked things around her to be done in an orderly fashion. One of her favorite sayings that followed us around the house was:

"There's a place for everything and everything in its place."

"But Mommie," I would retort.

"No buts," she would say, "Just do it, child."

"Scrambling around in chaos on the outside is a sure sign of chaos on the inside."

That was a powerful lesson that continued to occupy the center stage of my present lifestyle. Looking back on my life and the many cornerstones that were laid, I can see how extremely fortunate I have been being exposed to structure from an early age. Extremely creative, my mother's skills made her an excellent homemaker. She loved plants and cultivated them to adapt to indoor living. People from the community brought their struggling ferns to her for resuscitation. There were always living plants and flowers around to beautify the home and the garden. She had an ideal perspective on life's problems and a way of holding on to even the smallest bit of positivity to be found in any negative situation. This is another one of those traits I inherited from my mother. In her generation, women were not at all empowered, yet both my mother and my father understood the value of education and its ability to free women from bondage. She prayed diligently that her children would have the opportunity to be well educated.

My father on the other hand was a school teacher, one of the only eight certified school teachers in the country during the time of British rule. He was naturally intelligent and gifted with the skills of what I have now come to know as conflict resolution. The entire community leaned heavily on those skills. He was often called upon to mediate between families in land disputes and even in legal matters. He was not particularly a religious man—his philosophy in life was wrapped around living the "Christ" principles of loving your neighbor as yourself, forgiveness, peace, and grace. He often voiced his commitment to the church as attendance on the so-called holy days of the church—Good Friday, Easter, and Christmas. Outside of that, by my observation, he lived the Christ principles to the letter privately and silently by way of community involvement and the services he provided freely, without cost to all who needed it. This took him into the community to give his talents and his tithes in the care of others. He was well respected for his work in the field of education, opening the doors to a better life for both his students as well as their families. In his daily life, there was clear evidence of his compassion for the poor and needy. Despite all of these positive attributes, my Aunt Ette never forgave my father for what she called "ruining her sister's life" yet it would seem that these two had much in common. My father was the champion for education and civil rights while Aunt Ette was always on the side of the underdog, caring and outspoken. It was no surprise that she and her husband rose to the occasion on behalf of me and my mother.

Aunt Ette had an eye for fashion that in today's world, she would be recognized as the "fashionista" of the family. She stayed in the height of what was fashionable assisted by my mother who could replicate anything in the fashion world once she was shown a picture of it. I was blessed to be loved unconditionally by these two very special women. My mother, a beautiful woman inside and out, is compassionate, patient, caring, and overly religious. She was, it seemed, forever grateful to my aunt for her generosity and care for both of us. Much later in life, it was clear to me that my mother stayed praying at the foot of the cross for forgiveness and redemption. Her prayer life was all about seeking from God the forgiveness for her *sin* which she gave so freely to others. Her sin, in her eyes, was ever before her. I could see that she carried the rejection of the church as a weight on her shoulders that I sometimes felt was shifted to my own.

Throughout my childhood, I felt that I was under constant scrutiny by the community. This led me to become very observant and more often than not, too introspective. My love of nature and the joy it brought me when I was outdoors was compensation for an overly nosy community. The breathtaking beauty of a tropical morning is truly something to behold. The sun rising through the white mist of dawn was my childish vision of heaven. I was a dreamer and being in nature provided me with comfort and hope for bright tomorrows. My mother must have felt the same way too; she insisted that her entire household be out of bed before the rising of the sun. This was generally acceptable behavior in communities where there were farmers and even dock workers. My mother held us to the principle of rising with the sun. At my mother's first wake-up call, and there were usually three of these, by the third call, you knew you were in big trouble. I'd jump out of bed and head straight for the outdoors. The feel of the early morning dew under my bare feet invigorated me. Brushing my teeth outdoors to the backdrop of the rising sun peeping through the early tropical mist was my preferred way to greet the brand new day. On rainy daya I would try to get away with *being outdoors in the rain.*

Nature, it seemed, wrapped itself around me. I took it in and allowed the day's new energy to wash over my entire being. Early mornings seemed to provide me with a fresh feeling of love and comfort that made me ready to face the challenge each new day offered. Tropical sunsets also had a magical effect on me. Even as a young child I knew things, there was much however that I did not quite understand about the adults around me. For example, ome neighbor believe it or not, had twelve children. The husband it seemed was almost always beating the middle child in the back yard all the time. The adults around me wondered why it was he was always picking on this particular child. I was only about eight years old but I could "*sense*" the answer. The child was of a different energy make up than the others. He was not his so-called father's child. When I ventured an answer to my mother's repeatedly outspoken question. I was told to keep out of "grown folks" affairs. Much later in life when I began to practice meditation, I acknowledged that these feelings even at an early age was my natural ability to "*feel*" and "*sense*" at deep energetic levels.

The sun going down over a body of water brought thankfulness into my spirit. As a child, I truly believed that "God" dwelled somewhere between sunrise and sunset. There was a question that frequently occupied my childhood thinking—why did I not "feel" this same level of "sacredness" in the church building? I would ask my mother to explain the difference; she would try her best but her answer seemed never enough to satistfy my inbred curiosity. Guyana is called the land of many waters because of the abundance of rivers, lakes, and creeks. The sight and sound of large bodies of water also held me in "awe" bringing levels of peace and tranquility into what often felt like empty spaces in my life.

One particular joy for me was accompanying my mother or sometimes my aunt on early morning trips to the warf/fish market to purchase fresh fish. This was for me a special treat. I'd wander off to sit by the water's edge to enjoy the beauty of the early morning sun rising over the water. Fishing boats laden with the night's catch glided with perfect precision into the docks. An air of wonder would come over me as I took in the sights and sounds of what seemed to be a strange sort of organized chaos. Off-loading the catch of the night demanded every free hand and proceeded with care and precision. There was lots of free flowing dialogue—chit-chat flowing back and forth between the fishermen and the dock workers. It fascinated me to see women working right alongside the fishermen. It was hard work—sorting and lifting baskets of fish onto the hips and heads of the women. These images of women from the community hustling and bustling alongside the fishermen intrigued me. They were mothers and wives who in their homes played the subservient roles expected by husbands but who, with the sway of the hips and flow of playful banter, transformed themselves into skilled negotiators and aggressive businesswomen. They negotiated the wholesale prices for laden baskets of fish which were then parceled out and sold to the public at fish markets or simply by the side of the road.

It was my first acknowledgment of the strength and versatility with which we as women have been naturally endowed. The sights, sounds, and smells of the marketplace created for me a series of never-to-be-forgotten defining moments of my life. Here, men and women traders accepted and respected each other as equals in a way that was not possible in everyday life in a male-dominated third world country. By way of keen observation, these experiences honed and developed my people skills. I guess without quite knowing it, these images represented for me unique moments that taught me adaptability and the ever-present need to adapt to change. You could say that even as a child, spiritual truth, like a warm layer, always surrounded me. At the time, however, I was not mature enough to recognize it as such.

Soon, our little household moved to another Pentecostal church where there was love and acceptance. My mother began to unwind and ever so slowly allowed herself to become active in the life of the church. It made me so happy to see her smile when she was complimented for the quality of her voice or the solo she rendered so beautifully as only she could. She had found her voice and I was now blessed to wake up every morning to the beauty of her soprano voice greeting the morning. She sang half of the hymnal as she prepared all of the day's meals each day. Slowly, she seemed to crawl out of the shell of protection she had created around herself. She began to teach needlework classes to young girls. She even enthusiastically tried square and ballroom dancing and loved it. The church sponsored her for training at the Carnegie School of Home Economics where she graduated with a course certificate. My aunt and I were so proud of her and watched her share her skills with others and blossom. She had by indeed become a chef but would never have been given the official title because in old Colonial days, only men were considered to be chefs.

These skills opened up doors of opportunities for my mother to earn money. She was a natural organizer and so her organizing abilities led her to create a cottage business. She created beautiful wedding cakes and often catered for weddings and community celebrations. Another of her creative talents was making stuffed animals and trinkets which she sold to neighbors and folks in the community and thereby profited from the seasonal markets. She stayed busy, working with her hands well into the night to make attractive items for sale. As I grew older, my heart swelled with pride feeling the joy she experienced to be able to contribute financially to our upkeep.

In the meantime, weekly visits with my father were arranged and put in place. Accompanied by a female cousin, I visited my father's home on Sunday afternoons after Sunday School for about two hours. No one prepared me for my very first visit, what to expect, nor the atmosphere that I was about to engage—two vastly different households, much to see and learn, and an introduction to my father's wife. At the time, as I think back now, my father was perhaps a man in his mid-thirties, rather medium built, bald-headed, and clean-shaven. On my first visit, I entered the doorway into space that was well organized. The windows were open so that the room was sunny and airy. The first thing that caught my attention was the bookshelves along the wall, well stocked with books. Perched on a shelf, there was a radio. Lying on a couch in one corner of the room lay a woman. She looked very tired, her face drawn, she was sick, and did not seem to be able to move without assistance. He was a man that walked with an air of confidence. He was a school teacher, a graduate of the only teacher's training college, which in those days was the only doorway to enter into higher education. Career opportunities for black men in colonial days were extremely limited if not non-existent. Exposure to my father's circumstances and way of family life taught me much about order and the necessity to accept and flow with change. He was married. His wife, whom I grew to love, was a small, rather feeble woman. She was bedridden and had a voice so soft it was almost necessary to hold the breath to listen carefully to what she had to say. It was always positive. Strangely enough, she seemed to accept me in her home showing no resentment around the circumstances of my birth. She asked about my welfare, my performance at school, and always encouraged me to be an achiever. On my visits, I observed with great interest my father's mannerisms. He was a lover of classical and serious jazz music, so these sounds softly filled the air on Sunday afternoons.

Being in his space, I observed that he too was gifted with organizing ability as was my mother. Most importantly, I paid attention to and enjoyed being in his rhythm. Each visit brought questions to my mind most of which when voiced were answered roughly in the same way.

"If you live long enough, baby girl, you will come to understand."

"But . . . I need to know now." This was my constant answer.

"Everything you need to know is written in a book," my father would say.

"Read, child, that's where you will find most of your answers."

This created within me a love for books and I became an avid reader of any and everything I could get my hands on. Saturday afternoons at the library was another one of the outings that I thoroughly enjoyed. My father was a natural educator and I benefited tremendously from his peculiar form of using the surroundings as a natural stage for learning. It made me a serious observer and later, a debator in my school life. Teaching for him included home visits to the simple homes of his students to motivate the entire family. He encouraged parents who were illiterate to allow themselves to be taught in simple ways by their children. He showed keen interest in each of his students, often offering 'afternoon lessons' as it was referred to, free of charge to help them maintain their grades. There was no difference in his level of expectation of me and/or his students; we were encouraged to reach for excellence. The combination of these two environments to which I was exposed shaped my thirst for knowledge, made me an avid reader, and taught me how to adapt to change.

Strangely enough, after my trips to my father's house, my mother never questioned me about my father, my opinion, or his way of life. On that subject, it was like living with a wall of silence. At first, the lack of interest on her part bothered me. On the other side of that coin, my aunt would ask probing questions as she helped me to bed after each visit. Despite her silence, it was obvious that my mother studied my mood when I returned home. It crossed my mind that she was silently but duly checking to see if there was any discomfort for me being in the presence of my father's wife. At first, this perplexed me, but after a while, I adapted to the routine and accepted it for what it was. It made me an even keener observer and helped me to accept and embrace differences or diversity. At the end of each month, my father would give my cousin an envelope to deliver to my aunt, and being an inquisitive child, I knew it contained money that contributed to my upkeep.

Poverty, unemployment, and a high rate of illiteracy in British Guiana under British rule were the results seen all around us. As an educated black man in a colonial environment, my father knew and played his role well. People turned to him for leadership and he spent a great deal of his time writing letters on behalf of those who could not do it for themselves. He was always advocating for better conditions as well as providing representation to the disenfranchised, those in the community who could not speak up for themselves. As a child, I often wondered why people came to him to ask for legal representation when he was not a lawyer. I soon learned that he was part of a network of educated black males who were trained or groomed to educate and to be the voice for those who were marginalized. Later in life, he played a role in the thrust for independence and the liberation of British Guiana from the yoke of colonialism. As a teacher and community organizer, he was known for voicing this statement over and over again.

"Education is the key that leads us out of poverty."

"Well, not all the children in this country got a real chance to get an education, so what is to become of them?" I would ask, "the ones who cannot read or write?"

"Then it's the quality of conversation around that dinner table, hope, and stories of how we overcame the struggles of slavery that will move young minds," he would say.

"Parents have to talk about the pride they feel about the things that they do, show the joy of doing the things that are important to us as adults. This is what will move children and young people to get up and try harder."

Then he would go off into examples from his own childhood and having heard it so many times, I would try to shut out the sound of what I termed to be "old-time" talk and chatter.

"Some people do not know the power of excitement. God filled children with excitement for a reason. Us adults, we have to learn how to use it."

"You mean adults don't really know everything?"

I would ask sarcastically only to get that look that said quite clearly that I was out of order.

"Get children excited about learning new things and give them a good reason to copy what they hear and what they see; that's the beginning of the race to success."

"How so?" my mother would always ask.

"To teach a child is one thing; to excite the child's imagination, now that's another story."

In his role as a secondary school teacher, he moved a whole generation of poor children to literacy and beyond into higher education. I was exposed and nurtured by my father's philosophy, his way of life, and particularly his love of music. This taste in music was unusual in a community where calypso, with rather questionable lyrics, socca, and American pop hits were the trends of the day. His wife, a lady I never quite understood who was handicapped and bedridden, listened to the music played around her home. I watched silently as she was lifted from one place to another and wondered how she felt being so dependent upon others. She never complained, which surprised me since I was the "outside" child of my father. I had no way of knowing how she related to that when I was not around. To my presence, she showed no resentment and there were no awkward moments when I was around. She welcomed me into her home, enquired about my progress at school, and encouraged me to put my best foot forward at all times. She too never asked about my mother, my aunt, or my living conditions when I was not at my father's house. Throughout all of this, my mother stayed busy, remained silent, and never displayed haste or anger even as she dressed me for my visit to my father's house. In an attempt to hide/mask her real feelings, which she did well, she stayed busy. I have no memory of seeing my mother sitting idly. Her hands were always busy, knitting, sewing, tending to her precious plants, and taking care of her heart and home. She masked her feelings well, guarded her tongue carefully, and kept peace in the home. It was clear to me that she did have opinions about things around her; however, she kept her opinions to herself, never allowing her real feelings to be heard or seen. I had many questions but I followed my mother's lead, so I kept questions about my father to myself knowing that my aunt did not like my father one little bit. Most of my questions found their way into my journals even though at the time, I did not know they were journals. Reading and writing my thoughts felt very good to me.

School was all that my father as an educator, my mother, and my aunt expected of me. I was a quick learner and sometimes, a little too impatient with the slow progress of my schoolmates. I have to admit that despite all of the observations I did, I was not at all an over-friendly child. My love of and connection with nature provided for me comfort and tranquility so I did not create friends. In my own peculiar way, I was happy. You could say I had the advantage of living close to nature with two adoring mothers, my biological mother and my aunt. There was also the watchful community—they watched and waited for any sign that would prove the predictions of the elders to be right in my life. That in itself was more than enough attention for me. At the time, I did not know the real story of my conception and birth but could sometimes sense the depth of the pain my mother carried when I looked into her eyes. Every time I would attempt to ask my aunt questions about what worried my mother, my aunt's tone suggested to me that she was worried too. The times when I did muster up the courage to ask my aunt about my mother's silence, I would get that look with the accompanying words:

"You're a child, stay out of grown folks' story."

"I hear you, auntie, but . . ."

My aunt would gracefully turn away indicating the end of the line of questioning on my part.

So, I was surprised to discover that my mother worried a lot and took the time to voice her concerns about the absence of grandparents in my life. In the Guyanese tradition, grandparents are the cornerstones of family life. They live in the same household as their grandchildren; teach the oral history, trace the lineage, and culture of the family while they lovingly attend to the needs of each emerging generation. That attention included prayers and blessings enough to drown us children.

CHAPTER TWO

This void, the missing grandparents in my life, worried my mother and I could sometimes hear her talk in her prayer time to God about this concern. It became the source of serious, ongoing discussions between my mother and my aunt. Finally, with input from our new pastor, it was decided that a surrogate grandmother was indeed necessary. So, one Sunday afternoon, as soon as I returned from my visit to my father, I could feel my mother's excitement as she announced.

"Baby girl, I got good news for you today."

I caught the wave of excitement in her voice and prepared myself for the news.

"What, what is it, Mommy?" I asked joining into her excitement.

"Close the door."

I carefully closed the door anticipating the news that now held me in suspense.

"We found you a brand new grandmother."

"Who is we?"

I asked astonished, buying time to come up with a better comeback to this peculiar statement.

"Your auntie and me, we found you a grandmother."

I literally drew in a deep breath, swallowed hard, my mind racing ahead to determine what this really meant to my life. I never had a grandmother and could not see the need for one. In my opinion, grandparents were usually fragile, grumpy people who brought sickness into the house and I certainly did not need a real one never mind a make-believe one.

"What?" I exclaimed.

My thoughts were racing ahead to try to make sense of what I had just heard.

"Mommy! What are you saying?"

I retorted quickly, hoping to grasp her attention and change her mind before the idea could take root in her head.

"You don't just pick a grandmother, I never heard anything like that."

"There's a lot of things you never heard of at your age. Well, we just got you what you need most right now and it's a good thing."

"A good thing?" I was appalled.

The echo of what was said kept resounding in my ear and I was afraid in my mind as well.

I was truly perplexed; my reasoning mind hoped that maybe this was just one of those ideas that would fall through the creeks of life, using my aunt's expression. *Perhaps, it was a joke*, I thought. If it was a joke, I was not laughing because, to me, it was not at all funny. I even convinced myself that the whole idea would not go very far and that perhaps, I should just ignore it, but I could not get the idea out of my head. I hoped that if they kept talking about this so-called problem for a while, it could well phase itself out without the need for action, but then again, my aunt was known to be really persistent. The real fear was beginning to make itself felt as it clutched at my heart.

"My father was right," I blurted out before I could stop myself.

"Your father? How in the name of the Lord did he get into this conversation?"

My aunt was now livid with anger that I had dared to introduce my father's name into the mix. She did not like nor respect him, so to her, his views were irrelevant in any decision-making process in our lives.

"Who cares what he thinks or for that matter has to say? Like anybody would even ask him anyway."

"He says women do and say the craziest things that pop into their heads."

I ran the line so quickly I nearly choked on the words.

"Leave your father out of this. He ain't here and what he thinks or says doesn't have any place in this house, you hear me?"

I nodded my head to let her know that I had just heard what she said, but by no means did I agree with her sentiments. So, I straightened up, acknowledged to myself that I had just spoken out of turn, perhaps even made matters worse, and in so doing, lost any bargaining power I thought I might have had. My head was now swimming with thoughts and the more I thought about the problem, the more desperate I was beginning to feel. I knew, however, that I had to somehow get this idea out of my mother and my aunt's heads before it took root in the brain. I could see myself as the laughing stock of my schoolmates with a ready-made grandmother.

"This is weird," I grumbled to myself.

Summing up enough courage, clearing my throat, and in a pitiful voice, I murmured.

"I didn't ask for a grandmother."

One quick look at my mother's face and I knew that my comment was in no way helping my situation. I had slipped across that unspoken imaginary line adults create and call rudeness. So I lowered my head and held my silence. In my family, rudeness from a child addressed to an adult was considered one of the unforgivable sins. My mother's authoritative voice very quickly drew me back to the topic at hand.

"We'll get you together with your grandmother on Sunday."

"What . . . but Mom . . ."

"That's the end of this conversation, no more and's, if's, nor but's. Case closed."

Her tone told me clearly that the matter was non-negotiable. She turned away leaving me feeling desperate and teary-eyed. I turned my attention to my aunt who was standing close by taking in the scene playing out before her very eyes. I looked pleadingly into her eyes expecting to be rescued or at least, gain some sympathy. For my aunt, it seemed the matter was also resolved for she sighed and said in a well-controlled voice:

"Some arguments you win, some you lose. This one, you just lost."

"It's not fair. Nobody's listening to me right now," I said lamely.

"Now, you're right on that note. You're a child and you will do as you are told."

Then she looked at me with my head bowed, shoulders limp, and said in a soothing voice:

"Ah! you gonna like her; you two will get on like a house on fire."

I felt beaten down, dejected without even my beloved aunt on my side pleading for my case.

"Look at you worrying like some old woman. Stop it," she said.

"Maybe if I'm lucky, she won't like me," I grumbled halfheartedly.

This was an emotion that was totally unlike me. I was always accused by the adults in my life, including teachers, of being overconfident. So my aunt tried her best to reassure me.

"Oh, she will, don't worry about that."

With panic rising in my voice, I swallowed hard and asked:

"But if she doesn't, then what's next?"

I was growing more anxious by the minute feeling that there was no hope of rescue.

"You ask too many questions," my aunt responded.

I was beginning to wonder if this was about to turn into a game that teenage girls often played with flower petals. I could see myself doing it, dropping the petals in rhythm to:

"She likes me, she likes me not."

Over the course of the next week, anxiety forced me to spend every free moment I had sitting under my favorite mango tree trying to think my way out of what I considered a dilemma. I lost my appetite at the thought of another nosy old lady full of "wisdom" as grown-ups like to call it, entering into my life. The thought was frightening. I liked being by myself and was prepared to fight to keep this newcomer out, whoever she was. I did have to admit that I was now naturally curious about who the candidate might be. Even so, I was careful not to ask that question. Any inquiry about the name or identity of this person might be interpreted as interest or acceptance of the idea on my part. Just then, something I had heard my father say many times leaped into my mind, bringing a spring of hope.

"Women talk their way into things they cannot or will not finish."

"Please, God," I prayed aloud.

"Please talk them out of this one. Let this be the one they never finish."

So for the rest of the week, I continued to sit under my favorite mango tree hoping that there just had to be a way out. Sunday came and you could say that I was more than a basket case with worry. Nicely dressed for church, my mother and my aunt marched me across the street to the home of Mrs. Williams, as I always called her. She greeted us standing at her open front door.

"Baby," my mother said, addressing me in the voice she used when she was about to say something she considered important.

"Meet your new grandmother."

My mouth dropped open as I stared dumbly at the smiling, familiar figure of this elderly woman standing in the doorway. I was stunned. I did not expect the candidate to be so close to home. My newly assigned grandmother stretched out a feeble hand, smiled sweetly, and said:

"You and me, we gonna get to know each other real good."

I quickly stifled the thought that came into my mind.

Not if I can help it, I thought but was careful not to say it aloud.

She knew my name; everybody in our small community knew everybody else, their children, grandchildren, and as a matter of fact, the whole generation as well. She scrutinized my face for a welcoming response. There was none to be found.

"But first, my child, we're going down to the church house," she said almost absentmindedly.

"We got to ask God's blessing on this special walk you and me gonna take together."

"What do I call you?" I whispered.

The thought of calling anyone grandmother or granny was unthinkable. She looked down at me, smiled with a twinkle in her eye, and said.

"I'll take whatever you come up with."

"Miss Williams?"

I asked, a question mark clearly punctuating the two words. I searched her face for a reaction but her face was a blank sheet. Did she expect me to call her grandmother? So, to fill in the blank, I said under my breath:

"It's what I always call you anyway."

"That'll do for now," she responded and placed her arms around me.

Then, with my mother and my aunt beaming sunny smiles upon us, she took my hand in hers and we set out for the walk to the Sunday morning church service. I was convinced that our little party was being stared at from behind many closed doors and curtains.

So, as it turned out, my new relationship with this new grandmother was going to be interesting, to say the least. First of all, I thought that she lived a little too close for my own comfort. Keeping my nose close to the ground, I discovered that Miss Williams was the subject of whispers and gossips that I could not understand. She was ever-present on her porch or in her little garden early in the morning. I would wave to her when I left for school and she'd wave back. That was the sum total of my involvement with the old lady across the street. She seemed to be a lonely old woman and I wondered why it was that she had no children or grandchildren around her. Old people and children go hand in hand in our communities. Being an established elder in the church community, some people even considered her a relic of the church and the community. She did have the grandmotherly look with glasses perched on the tip of her nose and silky white hair which she wore in two plaits that fell to her shoulders during the week. On Sundays, however, she dressed in her Sunday best for church, let her hair down, and wore one of the most outrageous hats to be seen in the church. To me, she seemed ageless, a little unsteady on her feet but fiercely independent. Her face, though wrinkled, hinted the fact that she must have been a beautiful woman in her youth. I noticed how her face lit up with a special sparkle in her eyes when she smiled. I liked that about her and silently vowed that if there was no way out of this, I'd do my best to keep that light alive. If I was going to have me a grandmother, she would not be grumpy and mean like so many other grandmothers I had seen.

Everybody at church that Sunday morning had obviously heard the news and was well prepared to welcome us and celebrate the birth of what they called a union made in heaven. I was certainly not sure about that. The pastor called both of us up to the altar during the church service, blessed us, and the congregation provided the grand amen. At the end of the ceremony, it dawned on me that the die had truly been cast and I was stuck with her in my life. So I focused on my mother's promise to me and determined if there was any wisdom to be found, I would find it and grab some answers for myself.

"She has lived long enough, seen a lot in life, and probably have some good answers to those never-ending questions of yours," was my aunt's contribution to the saga.

"Really!" I interjected in response to what I considered a long-winded remark.

"Yes, she knows a lot. Don't you know she's a 'wisdom keeper' on the planet? You'd do well to listen and learn."

"A wisdom who, where do they come from?"

"Why don't you ask her about that? She'll tell you," my mother responded.

At first, I wasn't too convinced about the wisdom part because I soon discovered some interesting things about my new grandmother. The old lady possessed a sharp tongue and knew everybody's business including the history of my conception and birth. She had, it seemed, a reputation for saying exactly what was on her mind even to the pastor. To her credit, this was often offset by a unique sense of humor that allowed her to get away with things that were none of her business. There was, I discovered, also a bit of mystery surrounding the old lady. She was widowed and rumor had it that she had a grown son, but no grandchildren. This puzzled me and I began to think that the lack of children around her had something to do with whisperings in the community that I did not quite understand. The church and her beloved garden were the two focal points of her life until I came along. When she took my hand in hers, I could "feel" and sense her loneliness. This morning at church, her eyes seemed to light up matching the excitement in her voice when she talked about the joy and privilege she felt in being allowed to be my grandmother.

This is not so bad. It might work well, who knows, I thought silently.

Acknowledging that my fate had been well cast, I found myself vowing to do my best to keep that gleam in her eyes.

It'll give me something to focus on and pass the time away as well, I thought to myself. Those eyes of hers seemed to look deep into my very soul. At first, I was very uncomfortable in her presence but as the relationship grew, I saw the gleam of joy in her eyes particularly when I was being mischievous or just outright challenging. Having a grandmother was a brand new experience, but like every lesson I had to learn, I was catching on very fast. Miss Williams opened me up to a different kind of storytime; she never read stories from books as my mother did. We would sit on the porch as she created and narrated images of the "old days" as she called them, of the continent of Africa as told to her by her own grandmother who was a house slave. These stories delighted me; they were funny and did not dwell on the punishment and the bad times. I marveled at the strength of her memory. Her stories focused attention on the courage, faith, and bravery of the slaves in the face of trials and what she called tribulations.

"What's tribulations?" I asked curiously.

I had never heard the word before. She pulled her shawl around her frail arms as she seemed to gaze somewhere off the distance and each word carefully chosen was spoken with deep sorrow.

"That, my child, is when they think up every evil thing they can to frustrate you, to try to destroy the little faith that's keeping you going, and to bring shame and disgrace to you and your kin."

Here, I kept silent in honor of the sadness in her spirit.

"That's how we come to know God the way we do. With trials and tribulations, we have nowhere to turn but to Almighty God for comfort and strength."

I listened with great interest and watched her feeble body transform as she moved on to stories of faith and perseverance. These topics brought a hint of excitement back into her voice as she brought history alive in a most compelling way. She transferred within me the hope she felt for the future of my generation and the next. I ran errands for my newfound grandmother and helped around the house while she cooked delicacies that delighted my taste buds even though I did not care too much for her home-made soups. Throughout this getting-to-know each other period, I only ever met two members of her family—her very frail brother and a niece—these were the only ones remaining from her real family. The church members had become her adopted family; they took care of her and she was welcomed into our clan.

She sat proudly upright beside me at church, and we strolled back home with her holding my hands. I found it a little bit difficult to slow down my own pace to match her slower stride. She would question me about the sermon; no one else ever did that so I gave vague answers. My preoccupation was always trying to think through this strange, new addition in my life. She listened briefly to my skimpy responses to her question about the sermon, shook her head, and would say:

"You got to do better than that."

"What do you mean, Miss Williams?"

"You're intelligent enough to outsmart your classmates. Don't think I don't hear about your escapades at school. You can do better with your answers if you choose to pay attention."

The statement was said in a lighthearted way but behind it, I sensed that she would make me do better. So I began to not only listen to the sermons but to share my thoughts on what I was hearing. She'd listen to me, then smile knowingly as she added her own funny and often interesting take on the lesson. She was the only person I knew of who could add excitement to a sermon.

"Now, take Solomon and that Bathsheba woman."

She would preface her comment with a knowing sigh and a wink and then give me a funny or gossipy interpretation of the story.

"How do you know it was that way?" I would ask playfully.

"When you live as long as I have, you come to know a little something."

"You know more than a little something, Grandma."

I had now moved with confidence to calling her Grandma and I could feel her delight whenever I did. Her face would light up at the utterance of the word and it was becoming very clear to me how much we needed each other. We shared the same love for the outdoors and we both listened to and struggled to understand the pastor's sermons. However, I liked her interpretations of the scripture better than the pastor's version. It seemed to me that the little "something" as she put it was often a lot bigger than she made it out to be. This led me to wonder how she came to know things the pastor did not seem to know. I began to realize that when I was in her presence, questions would often jump into my mind with a pressing need for answers, and this would cause me to fidget.

"Sit still, child," she would say. "What's wrong with you?"

She had always encouraged me to speak the truth no matter what the consequences so I would respond.

"Why? I don't want to."

"You got to learn how to sit in your own rhythm, baby"

"Why?" I would ask.

"Because, baby, it is good for you to learn how to do so. Life's better in your own rhythm."

I resented being called a baby and practiced ways to let her know of my resentment without being disrespectful. It took me years after she was gone for me to fully understand what she meant by "sitting in my own rhythm." This became one of her sayings that has remained with me throughout my life and has pushed me to understand the term rhythm. It required a great deal of work and practice later on in my life; it was a not-so-easy task to master sitting in one's own rhythm. Now, it has become one of the centerpieces of my foundation from where I conduct life coaching sessions. My grandmother was also truly a prayer warrior extraordinaire. Members of the church community knew this and brought their woes, worries, and concerns to her for counseling and prayer. In turn, I often heard her talk to God aloud asking for his mercy and grace particularly when her hands were busy in the garden or while cooking a meal in the kitchen. I was intrigued by the way she consistently asked God for mercy.

"Father God, we asking for your mercy."

"Why do you keep asking God for mercy? They need help."

"Because mercy has everything we need—love, acceptance, forgiveness, and don't forget healing of course."

"You really think so, Grandma."

"Yes, I know so."

The conviction in her voice when she said those words touched me and made a believer in me. Now I know that these are words of comfort and truth and try to remember them not only in times of my own distress but when I have to comfort others. In my own life, I have acknowledged that my faith was strengthened by the wellspring and essence of the words of wisdom from the elders around me, including my grandmother. As children in the community, we were recipients of their grace and wisdom and sometimes chastisement as well to keep us on the straight and narrow way of life. After such exercises, we would be told:

"Chastisement is good for the soul, we got to bend the tree while it is still young."

Needless to say, we as children did not agree with the statement and prayed for a less painful and acceptable way to bend the tree that is destined to become our lives. Then, she would toss this one into the mix:

"Always remember, no matter what life throws at you, God is in charge."

As a child, I noticed that her prayers did not particularly remove the burden in the lives of those who sought her out for prayers. They arrived distressed yet they left with a peculiar calm that seemed to bring them comfort and peace. Sometimes, I'd see a miracle in response to her prayers. For an old woman, she was very busy bringing comfort to those in grief, counseling the young, praying diligently for the sick/distressed, and attending funerals. Today, when I look back on her life and her front porch with its two rocking chairs, I see the equivalent to a modern-day psychologist couch. After the "seekers," those who sought her out would leave, I'd hear her cry out to God.

"Let thy will be done, thy will be done, Lord."

It was her way of bringing closure to her intervention on behalf of others. These were the circumstances and the statements that grabbed my attention, which became embedded deep in my consciousness very early in my life. Later in my life, these words framed a series of questions that played out in my mind for many years and which demanded answers. Living out the above led me to yet another question that would jump into my mind when she and I talked about prayer.

"If he is in charge and all is well, why is there so much suffering in the world?"

"You paying more attention than I give you credit for," she would say.

". . . and why is the whole church, including the Pastor, telling God what to do?"

At this line of questioning, she would turn to me with the most perplexed expression in her eyes.

"Your turn, gimme the answer to that last part, I'm baffled too."

"I don't know the answer, that's why I'm asking," I would say pleadingly.

"Child, people got to be taught how and what to talk to God about."

"How so, they don't know?"

"Most of the time, I think they really don't know. You won't go to the Queen of England's house and tell her what to do, would you?"

"No, ma'am, I don't think so, they won't let me in."

"You know so. Then, tell me why people respect her more than they respect Almighty God."

My little mind could not stretch that far to even begin to conceive an answer so I remained silent.

I did know that everyone in the church, including the pastor, seemed to me to be begging God for a whole lot of things that they wanted. My grandmother went to God to ask that his will be done in the lives of her seekers. So, I took a deep breath and asked the next burning question on my mind.

"Did you ask God for a grandchild?"

Her response was immediate without any serious thought.

"No, I didn't."

She responded shaking her head from side to side to reinforce her answer.

"Well, did you want one?"

We fell into a wall of silence for a while, then quite unexpectedly, a beautiful smile crossed her face, and with that twinkle in her eyes, she said:

"That's one of those blessings I didn't know I needed. God gave it to me anyway and now here you are, one of the joys of my life."

"Can I ask you another question that's kinda bin on my mind too?"

"You already on a role, ask away, what is it?"

I scrutinized her face carefully to see if the timing was right for my question.

"How come there's a picture of your son in the drawing-room, but I never see him come to the house to visit and you never talk about him at all?"

We were doing dishes. She paused, looked down at me, and the pain was visible in her eyes. She put the dish in her hand carefully on the countertop. Wiping her hands on her apron, she reached out, took me by the shoulders, and sat me down on the nearby stool. The pain I saw in her eyes slowly crept into her voice.

"Some things we just don't ever talk about."

"Not even to God? You say we can talk to God about everything."

She sighed, took a moment to compose herself, and then continued.

"Me and God, we do talk about my son a lot and I leave it there and you should too."

Now there was anguish in her voice, the spark left her eyes which made me regret asking her the question in the first place. I vowed silently to myself to leave that mystery alone for as long as we were in each other's company. It seemed to me that she didn't ask God for a grandchild, yet here I was, large as life. Maybe God will fix whatever it is. The thought raised another question in my mind. However, I sensed that as my mother would say:

"Leave that thought well alone."

My new grandmother turned out to be an excellent storyteller. Her stories delighted me because they came directly from the heart. I sat with bated breath as she painted for me images of Africa the motherland as it was given to her by her grandmother who was a house slave. It turned out that her grandmother was given the stories from her own grandmother. These were stories of perseverance, strength, and the survival of black people living in exile outside of the motherland. These stories were about the roots of black people, pride, ritual, and celebration in the motherland. Optimism was sown deeply into my spirit and has left me being an eternal optimist because of her. I gleaned not only from her stories but also from the levels of love expressed in the tone of her voice. She schooled me well on the slaves' struggle to keep a semblance of a family together both during and soon after slavery. Through her eyes, I experienced slavery as a heroic feat on the part of the slaves. Developing and maintaining pieces of a cherished oral tradition under extremely hard and painful times required and demanded courage. She left me spellbound when she told the stories of selflessness of those who risked losing their own lives to save the lives of those who were part of the underground movement. Saving just one life among the loss of thousands seemed to matter in those perilous times. Our ancestors' dedication to passing down the little they could of heritage, lineage, and spiritual practices by way of the oral tradition moved me deeply. Keeping "family" rooted in the minds of the slaves and the hope of somehow being able to establish a community in a strange land were major goals of their survival. These stories of courage, faith, and perseverance touched me deeply. It shaped my historical point of views around slavery as well as my philosophical views on life. My grandmother would say with such deep emotions:

"They kept it together, they sure did, they kept it together."

"Times were rough then, but they kept it together with the help of Almighty God."

These words came out of her with pride that was transplanted into my own spirit. Keeping it together were the words that ended every one of those stories from the "old days" that she shared with me.

Later in my adult life, during my own middle passage of trials and tribulations, these words would rise up in my very soul. These became precious words reminding me that there is always a way to endure disaster and/or withstand trials and tribulations and yet overcome. Long after she was gone, when I found myself swimming against the tidal wave of life and when pain and disaster struck, these words became the cornerstones of my faith and my own survival. Every statement has become for me a piece of the foundation upon which my "knowing" of what love is was at its most primal level. Later, when I was blessed with children, my own parenting skills were grounded on the morals that came out of the stories I was blessed to receive from her. Soon after this faith/prayer warrior came into my life, I was faced with my first very deep loss. My beloved aunt lost her husband in a car accident. I was alone with her when the messenger brought the news to her front door that her husband had just been struck by a car and was hospitalized with serious injuries. She quietly received the news and determined to investigate the matter before crying out to the community. We crossed the road and asked for prayers from my grandmother, then she and I proceeded to the hospital. I do believe at this point she was hoping that it was a case of mistaken identity. Later that same evening, he died without regaining consciousness.

The grief in our little family was devastating and many-fold. It was in fact, loss of a husband to my aunt, loss of a father figure to me, loss of a family member to whom my mother was very grateful, and loss of the provider of the family. I watched the spark of light in my aunt's eyes go out when the hospital staff pronounced her husband dead. She was grief-stricken and became a shadow of her old self as I watched her enter into a wall of silence that was so unlike her usual outgoing, take-charge-of-everything self. She moved as if in a trance and I felt helpless in acknowledging that neither myself nor my mother seemed to be able to reach her in her grief. The owner of the car involved in the accident showed up at our home that evening. He was a white, British man and it was the first time anyone in our community had ever seen a white man or woman visit our community. He brought his condolences, apologized on behalf of his driver who was driving at the time of the accident, and offered to pay the funeral expenses. It was extremely good of him to do so and gave me a new insight into race relations at that time in my country. My aunt continued in her grief and had lost weight rapidly. Neighbors and church members were a great help but the rest of the family stuck to their role of being non-participants in our lives. She mourned the loss of her husband for an entire year wearing only black.

My mother who was distraught tried her best to comfort her and to be of assistance, singing hymns of comfort at daybreak to help my aunt out of her grief but to no avail. My newfound grandmother became a tower of strength to both my mother and my aunt. She spoke soothing words of wisdom hoping to fill the void. I cried silently in my bed for days and nights in my own grief at the loss. In anguish, I asked my grandmother the question:

"How could a good God do this to us?"

"The Lord gives; the Lord takes away."

This was the response from my grandmother. She held me close and allowed me to cry myself to sleep, then I awakened to hear her praying aloud over my sleeping body. When she realized that I was awake, these were the comforting words she said to me:

"What I do know, baby, he makes things right in the end."

These were her last words to me on the subject. I did not exactly feel comforted by those words at the time, but in my little heart, I kept on praying:

"Please, God, bring the joy back into my auntie's eyes."

Two years after the death of her husband, my auntie received a gentleman suitor who respectfully approached the pastor of the church to ask permission to propose marriage to my aunt. Yes, it was the way things were done in the old days. He received permission and "Dad" as we all called him became the grandfather figure in my life. I watched in awe the spark of light return into my auntie's eyes. Everyone, including my mother, was guarded about the prospect of this proposed marriage. The community, of course, had a lot to say; most of it not so good. In the times in which this proposal was made, widows seldom remarried. Two widowed, lonely middle-aged people stepped into the church on a Monday morning for a quiet ceremony supported by three family members. My aunt married her second husband. I saw the joy in her eyes and knew that God had indeed answered my prayer. I was beginning to grow faith.

By the age of twelve, I surrendered my life quite unexpectedly to Christ at a tent revival conducted by the little white church allegedly built by slaves. Every Sunday, we would pass this little church and I would marvel at the fact that those pews were occupied in the past by our black ancestors. I'd listen to our pastor's sermons in our church and wonder about the types of messages that motivated people who suffered so much. Soon, I began to write down questions that arose in my mind from the sermons preached on Sundays and to seek answers from those around me.

"Why did a good man have to die to save us from sin?" I asked the pastor.

"Because he loved us," was the answer.

"Does that mean that people who love me will have to pay for my sins?"

"You silly child, the answer to that question is no."

"No? So explain to me how does that really work?"

"Hush, be quiet and listen, child."

When I asked the same question in Sunday school, the teacher's response was:

"You're in church—the house of God, time to praise him. Enough of your questions."

With those words came that stern look from the teacher that was intended to stop my questioning or even maybe my thinking.

"Yes, maam."

I would bow my head in embarrassment feeling that I had once again asked a disrespectful question. My frustration mounted in the absence of real answers. It raised for me a multitude of other questions that also demanded answers. After attendance at two funerals in a row, I voiced yet another bothersome question.

"Didn't Christ say that he came to give us life more abundantly?"

"Yes he did, do you believe him?" my Sunday school teacher responded.

This was one of my most persistent questions. No one seemed to have an answer to this particular one.

"How come people are still dying since he left us?"

A hushed silence fell among the adults in the room. There seemed to be no answer to that one, too, and I was disappointed once again.

The hardships and effects of poverty in the communities surrounding my life were stark and brought out raw emotions in me. Growing up in a poor community, there were families all around us that were really in need. We did not have a lot but we always had food. So one day, I asked the pastor:

"When are you going to take a few fish and bread, bless it, and feed all these hungry people around us?"

"What do you mean?" he demanded.

I sensed agitation in his voice and wondered if I had again overstepped my boundaries as my mother would say.

"Is that not what Jesus did?" I asked innocently.

"He said anything he did we can do also," I continued.

This one resulted in my mother using that stern voice that let me know without a doubt that I was being disrespectful. She determined that my persistent questioning was becoming an embarrassment to the family. So I stopped asking questions and focused my attention on recording my questions in my notebook. I certainly did not see my questions to be provoking, and I was really just seeking answers to questions that troubled me. So I stopped the questioning and diligently wrote my questions down on paper hoping to find someone, somewhere, at some time with the ability to provide answers to these pressing questions. Soon after this action, I turned a corner so to speak, and once again faced the tragedy of death; only this time with more than the usual accompanying drama.

Around the tender age of eleven, there was a loud knock on the front door. I opened it to find a male elder standing there, hat in hand.

"Go get your auntie." There was a degree of urgency in his voice.

That knock on the door brought the news that my father's wife had died. I searched for my mother's face for a response. There was nothing to see; she remained stoic. I was very sad for Auntie Maude as I called her and for my mother who stayed so silent throughout the days leading up to the funeral. Everyone, it seemed, had an opinion or two about this new "situation" as they referred to it. My aunt and her new husband made the decision that I would be taken to the funeral by my cousin who at the time was ten years my senior. Even at eleven, I expected a family discussion around the circumstances of my life. If there was one, I was certainly not privy to it. It seemed odd to me that life continued in much the same pattern of weekly visitations on Sunday with my father; only now, he and I had more time to spend together outdoors. I waited nervously for any signs that this change of status would bring yet there was nothing but gossip all around me. My father was quiet and seemingly contemplative; my mother never brought up the subject but I could tell from her body language that she was thinking and wondering too. This clouded and heavy environment continued around me for nine months without communication between my parents.

Nine months after his wife's burial, I responded to yet another knock on the front door. Upon opening it, I was shocked to see my father standing there. This was very new to me; I had never seen my father at our house before. I also knew how my aunt felt about him and was sure that he would not be welcomed.

"Baby girl, is your aunt home?"

He asked the question in what seemed to me like a very strained tone.

"She's home," I said.

I found myself in grave discomfort not knowing for sure what to do next.

"Go, go, get her."

Having been told that it was rude to close the door on an adult, I stood there unsure of what my next move should be.

"It's okay," my father said gently ushering me to close the door between us.

"Close the door, I'll wait out here," he urged.

I had never seen my father nervous before and my heart went out to him.

I closed the door gently, turned, and almost collided with my aunt.

"Whose at the door?"

I could not bring myself to answer that question, so I stepped past her while my eyes transfixed on the closed door.

"Child, you forgetting your manners?" she chided me.

"Somebody outside, why you close the door?"

Nervously, I stepped around her, pulled the door open, and stepped back waiting for the verbal explosion I expected to happen.

"Oh! It's you," my aunt said in her most disapproving tone.

"What you doing on my doorstep?" she asked suspiciously.

My father looked very apologetic and in a soft voice, he addressed my aunt calling her by her name.

"Ethel, you know my wife died."

"That ain't no secret, everybody knows that," was her icy response.

"What do you want?" Her hands moved to her hips.

Before he could answer the question, she rudely interjected.

"I can't understand why you don't know you're not welcome here," my aunt said.

"That may be so, but we need to have a conversation about my baby girl's future."

"She fine, I got no worries."

The tone of her voice indicated that as far as she was concerned, the verbal exchange was over. My father was a big advocate of standing up for one's rights, even though he always insisted that it should be done with respect. I knew that he was not about to give up on this fight so I took a deep breath and waited. Clearing his throat, he said:

"I kept the traditional mourning period of nine months after my wife's death and I am now ready and able to pick up on my responsibilities."

My aunt stared back blankly at him for a moment, then raised her voice:

"And what the hell do you mean by that?"

Looking around nervously, my father responded:

"Ugh . . . the neighbors are watching."

"So, let them watch, you come here and start all this."

"Can we talk like two adults inside of the house?"

"I never say you can come in."

She looked him up and down as if contemplating whether or not he was worthy of entering her home. After what seemed like an awkward silence, she relented and seemed to me to soften up a little. My father, seizing the moment of hesitation on the part of my aunt, pressed his point.

"Can I come in to discuss this important matter?" he asked cautiously, his hat respectfully held in his hand.

My aunt rolled her eyes, looked heavenward as if seeking help from above, sighed heavily, and reluctantly stepped aside. My father entered the living room cautiously, to my surprise, he was offered a seat. My mother, who I was sure was within earshot, was nowhere to be seen. As it turned out, she was not invited to participate in this initial conversation. Even at my tender age, I acknowledged that an important element of my mother's life was about to be debated and it seemed she would not have a voice in the discussion or, for that matter, the outcome. For some reason, I did not quite understand why I felt so sad for her. I was asked to leave the room and I did. My aunt kept her eyes on me until I walked down the stairs and out of earshot. Even in my childhood state of innocence, I knew that something was not right with the scene I had just left.

"Please, God, make it right," I pleaded under my breath.

The pastor of the church we were attending at the time was duly invited to round two of the discussions and to another meeting that followed. I was sent across the street to my grandmother's house to keep my inquisitive mind, as my aunt called it, out of grown folks' business.

"Don't look so worried," my grandmother said scrutinizing my face.

"I . . . I don't understand," I stammered, shaking my head from side to side.

"Hush, of course, you don't, me neither, but I got a feeling that God is about to showcase his mercy right before our eyes."

"You think so, grandma?"

"I know so. Everything's gonna be all right."

I certainly did not feel in my heart the same level of confidence that she displayed.

Together, we watched the house from behind the blinds in grandma's house. About an hour later, my father left the house and my grandmother took my hand and led me across the street to our home. I know she was expecting to be invited in but my aunt thanked her at the front door, bade her goodbye, and gently closed the door. The result of all the discussions was that my parents gained permission to speak to each other and to determine whether there were enough "feelings" for a relationship. The look on my mother's face and the spark in her eyes told me all I needed to know. Soon, my father and mother were allowed to re-enter the relationship they started so many years ago. I was happy with the decision and ready to live the rest of my life without the unspoken tension that haunted my early childhood. My aunt, on the other hand, was not at all happy with the result but thankfully, her new husband, an educated and intelligent man, got her to see reason. So began the second half of my childhood with my father fully present in my life. Two brothers followed; I have to admit that I was a bit jealous and felt that each one when they arrived on the scene had intruded into my personal space.

My newfound grandmother helped us all through the joy and tragedy as my aunt called it. Adjustment to the new status of being a big sister was not easy as life with its series of interesting twists and turns continued. My mother was so much more relaxed and I could sense that these two really liked each other and that was a good page in my book. The rest of the family, my uncles and aunts, however, continued with their lives with the same arrogance and detachment as if the reunion had never happened. The neighbors, of course, had much to say. Looking back on the memory of that episode in my life, I realize that since the country had no television at that time, gossip was in fact the equivalent of a soap opera and did they enjoy it. I adjusted quickly to the changes. School for me continued to be a breeze, the upside to my inquisitive mind. That which drove everyone around me crazy made learning easy for me. My parents were talking to each other and my grandmother was happy about the reunion but my aunt, on the other hand, was surly. For me, my growth and development were moving along quite steadily and to my satisfaction so I prayed for my aunt to get in line with progress I was feeling.

I entered high school and another one of my major challenges began. My father was an English teacher at the high school I was scheduled to attend. On the morning of my first day at high school, my father gave me an interesting take on learning and set guidelines I was expected to follow.

"I am sending you to school," he said looking me in the eye.

"To a place where there are adults and teachers who have information and wisdom in their heads. It is your task to very quickly find a way to transfer the knowledge they have from their brain into yours."

I was standing there very respectful but in my mind, I was thinking that I was going to school to be taught, so I kept my mouth shut. I never looked at it the way he had just presented it to me, so I pondered this statement for all of my high school years. Next, he said:

"I personally do not believe there is any value in corporal punishment. I do not beat you or any of the children in school. That's my personal preference."

I was happy to hear this because whipping by teachers was an acceptable punishment in the school system at that time. My delight soon turned into dismay with his next statement:

"Learn the rules, follow them carefully, do not expect me to save you from a whipping from teachers who believe in the value of discipline by way of corporal punishment."

I disagreed with this sentiment but was acutely aware that this conversation was one of those where he talked; I was supposed to listen and take note.

"You are my seed, I expect you to lead not follow. Do you understand that?"

"Yes sir," was my whispered response.

"In terms of grades, I expect nothing but the best. Anything less will result in disciplinary measures. Got that?"

"Yes sir," was my rapid-fire response this time.

In the second term of high school, I brought home a report card that graded me third place in a class of thirty-five students. I knew I was in trouble and dragged my feet all the way home expecting the worst. I presented him with the report card (the contents of which he already knew because he had access to the school's report cards). I braced myself for the inevitable that would surely include his own, very creative way of punishment. I expected, for example, to be banned from every special occasion in the family and in the community. I anticipated that the usual fun month-long August trip to the countryside and the beach would be lost to me. He read the contents of the report card aloud twice. Then, he scrutinized me as if I was some sort of alien, and with a puzzled look on his face, he said:

"You are my seed, how in the world did you manage this?"

I was perplexed. This was not the response I expected. Before I could think of something to say, he continued.

"You worked really hard to override what's in your makeup. You, my child, are you not?"

"I . . . I don't know what to say," I stammered.

My father being an English teacher, we were not allowed to shorten words in the English language. I had just committed the second fatal sin in the family.

"There is no such word as don't," he exclaimed.

"Remove yourself from my presence," he said in controlled anger.

To which I responded by scampering out of his presence. To my surprise, no punishment was administered. I avoided him as much as I could throughout the August school holiday. However, each time we came face to face at the meal table, he would look me in the eyes and say:

"How in the world did you manage to accomplish such a disgraceful feat?"

"You had to have worked really hard at it."

The discomfort and embarrassment I felt throughout the month of August ensured that I did not fail in my responsibility to deliver what was expected of me. I maintained my grades at the top of the class and did ensure that I did not drop below his expectation. Many lessons around genealogy, parental responsibility, and psychology were all taught to me by him that year. As my father put it:

"Parents have the responsibility to pass on good genes. I did that."

"You've been taught good values. What in the world is wrong with you?"

"I expect at this phase of your life at least three times more than what has been put into you."

This account of his expectation of me scared the devils out of me. *Who could possibly accomplish three times more than he had in his lifetime?* I asked myself.

My mother was silent. It was clear that her respect for my father would not allow her to challenge anything he said or did; at least not in the presence of us children. She was very proud, even if she did not say so in front of my aunt, of the reputation my father had in the community—for speaking his truth even in the face of ridicule and for being a strong and caring community leader whom everyone respected. My aunt, on the other hand, never forgave my father for what she considered as the shame he brought upon the family name.

When I asked my newfound grandmother what she thought about my aunt's opinion, her response surprised me.

"Your auntie is as stubborn as a mule. She refuses to take a sip from the cup of forgetfulness."

Since I was raised by my mother to believe that forgiveness was the key that opened heaven's door, I was horrified at the thought of my aunt going to hell.

"What does that mean?" I asked with concern.

"Does it mean she's going to hell? Is God going to punish her?"

"That, my child, is not your question or mine to ask. Just keep praying for your auntie."

CHAPTER THREE

Life with all of its topical twists and turns continued. My "coming of age" as it was referred to in our community was celebrated with a "rite of passage" ceremony conducted by my great aunt Sarah. No one, not even Aunt Sara, knew her true age. She had no birth certificate so her age was determined from the memories and stories that she shared, particularly the ones told to her by her grandmother who was a slave. This ceremony of "rites" was handed down orally through the generations by the African ancestors. In the countryside of Guyana, it was practiced mainly by country folks who sought to maintain what elements of tradition they had gleaned from the elders. It was a celebration of the coming of age of a young woman when she experienced her first menstrual period. Over the years, it had developed into an adaptation of the original African concept. In its redesign, the African practice of mutilation was removed to be replaced by elements of God's love and redemption of the newfound faith of the black community. So, it was that on a moonlit night the community gathered. Aunt Sara who rarely left her village traveled to the city on this occasion to conduct the ceremony.

It was a beautiful ceremony of "thanksgiving and praises" to Almighty God for bringing me onto the threshold of womanhood. Traditional African songs of praise and thankfulness were sung amidst prayers to Almighty God for blessings upon my head as I journeyed through to womanhood. Aunt Sara also extended blessings on all who were present in the same way she had received the ceremony instructions from her elders. The ceremony proceeded with a serious mother/daughter talk at which my aunt was present to support my tearful mother throughout the process. My mother shared with me her anxiety and fear during the labor/delivery process. Soon after her baby was born, she was told the spiritual meaning of the "caul" that covered my face at birth. It signified to the elders, she said, a child born with sight into both the spiritual and physical worlds. She confessed her feelings of total inadequacy at sixteen years of age to raise a child that was considered "gifted" at birth. My aunt then instructed me in a very tender voice on what it meant to be a woman.

"My child, the most sacred place on earth is inside the womb of a woman. Guard this sacred space with your life and be mindful of who or what you allow to enter in there."

"It is the place where God and man meet to create new life. It's a big responsibility that God put upon our lives as women to be part of creation and to allow us to nurture new life in and out of the womb."

I felt quite numb and at a loss for words and wished my paternal grandmother was present who I was sure would have been able to make all these words make sense.

"Women are the caretakers and nurturers of future generations," my aunt continued.

"As women, the way we are and the way we raise our children is the gift or otherwise that which we give to the world."

I did not quite understand all that was said that day but the tenderness of my aunt's voice and my mother's silent tears wrapped a cloak of sacredness around me. That beautiful feeling of warmth and comfort was re-experienced by me at the birth of each of my children.

CHAPTER FOUR

At the age of twelve, I spontaneously surrendered my life to Christ. It is the only important step that I can recall that I made alone without any consultation from my immediate family or even my newfound grandmother. It happened on a sunny weekday on my way home from school. There was a tent revival, an open-air meeting in the community. As I recall, it was the only thing I have ever done all by myself without the support of members of my small family. The preacher, after a very powerful sermon on redemption, made an altar call to his listeners. Standing on the side of the road across the street where the service was held, I felt goosebumps all over my body when the preacher put out the call to sinners to step forward and ask and receive redemption and turn over the life to Christ. I was in tears when I felt myself walking very confidentially to the makeshift altar where I stopped and proceeded to prostrate myself on the ground at the feet of the pastor. There were others kneeling there but I was the only one who seemed to have dropped to the ground, arms outstretched, and rendered my body as a cross. Members of the congregation as well as the pastor prayed over me. It was a life-changing experience. When it was over, my girlfriend and I walked slowly in silence to my house.

"How are you going to tell your straightlaced family that you surrendered at a tent revival meeting?"

"I don't know," I responded shaking my head.

I was aware that I had just created a bit of a problem. You see, my father disapproved of what he called "hysterical sermons" intended to get people all stirred up emotionally.

"I wish you luck getting your father to understand this one."

I arrived home, dropped my books, and raced over to my grandmother's house to get her opinion on how to tell this extraordinary story to my parents. She looked up from her task of watering the house plants.

"My, my, where's the fire? Slow down, child."

I was so out of breath I could not respond immediately.

"Slow down, child, now take a deep breath, what's the matter?"

"I got something to tell you," I gasped.

"Out with it, I'm listening," she responded.

"I got saved today."

I scrutinized her face for a reaction to the news. She, however, silently continued with the task at hand as if what I had just said was quite natural.

"So, where did you get this idea in your head that you were not saved before?"

Ignoring the question, I excitedly shared my experience at the revival service. When I was finished outlining the circumstances, her response was not what I expected.

"Hmmm," she said as she picked up the watering can and continued tending her favorite maiden-hair fern plant. In the ensuing awkward silence, I searched her face for a clue as to what she was really thinking—there was silence that fell heavily between. In the silence I could "feel" that she approved.

"Hmmm."

"Is that all you got to say?" I retorted with disappointment.

"You did well."

I could tell she choose those three little words very carefully as if to say that there would be no further conversation on the matter.

"But . . . we belong to the Anglican Church," I retorted.

"So, God ain't picky, he takes Anglicans too."

"But . . . what do I say to the Priest, my mother, oh my God, my father?"

"God appoints and he got ways and means to let his wishes be known."

"You not helping me here—you think so?"

"I know so."

She dismissed any further questions in her own special way by quietly singing the opening lines from a hymn.

"Only believe, only believe, all things are possible, *only* believe."

I entered her house with haste and excitement but my journey across the street felt like a mile long and I engaged it slowly and painfully. Behind me, she kept singing.

I could hear the echo of her voice in my ear as she sang. I crossed the street and slipped in our back door hoping no one would hear me enter the house. My mother was preparing the evening meal.

"Where were you? Your books here but you nowhere to be found."

"What's wrong? You don't look so good?"

My mother looked at me up and down as if searching to find where the exact problem was that caused me to enter and leave the house without a greeting.

"I was across the street. I'm just tired, just tired."

"Well, get your homework done, my child."

At dinner time, I had no appetite and my mother placed her hands on my forehead to determine if I was coming down with something.

"Well, you don't have a fever, what's wrong with you?"

I went to bed trying to figure out how my life would change, but more importantly, how my father would react to this piece of news.

The following day, Pastor David from the Pentecostal church visited the house to share the good news of my salvation and invite the entire family to join the Pentecostal church. Needless to say, my aunt who happened to be visiting our home and my mother were hearing all this for the first time. I suspected that my father had already heard the news by way of the grapevine. He graciously thanked Pastor David for his visit and quite politely gave the pastor an assurance I am sure he did not expect to or want to hear.

"We are Anglicans, we have no intention of changing religion."

Much to my surprise, the topic was not discussed any further. My father had spoken and so it was. We continued in the usual way with our lives and our chosen way of worship.

Soon after that, Aunt Sarah paid us a surprise visit from the country to deliver what she called a prophecy. It was during the full moon when families gathered under the light of the moon to tell stories, enjoy home-cooked food, and play games. Aunt Sarah's presence was a special occasion on this particular night. She pulled her shawl tightly around her slender shoulders and speaking directly to me, she said:

"My child, I've come to tell you what the angel whispered into my ear."

"You have a "calling" on your life to minister to and shepherd people. You will go to far-off lands, and leave your mother, father, and family behind you. Your ministry will touch many lives in many very peculiar ways."

I was dumbfounded. At this time in my life, I was extremely shy and could not get it together to even make friends. It seemed to me that her prophecy had little hope of being fulfilled. Now, on the other hand, Aunt Sarah was known for her prophecies that came to pass. This aspect bothered me immensely since I could not and had never dreamed of ministry in my life. Later when we all headed back indoors, my mother and I were doing the dishes and I timidly brought up the topic.

"Why did Aunt Sarah say what she said about me?"

My mother searched my face as she continued with the task at hand. There was a pregnant silence between us and I can sense my mother processing silently what Aunt Sarah had said very carefully. I knew I had to speak up and let my feelings be known on the subject at least to my mother. I summoned up enough courage to say:

"I don't want to be a preacher. Whoever seen a woman preacher in a pulpit?"

My mother gave me the benefit of her full attention. The next words that came out of her mouth baffled me. With a sigh, she said:

"The stone which the builder reject may well become the head cornerstone."

"I don't want to be a preacher. I want to be a teenager," I protested.

The words rushed from my head to my lips before I could stop myself from uttering them.

My mother very carefully set the dish in her hand aside, untied her apron strings, and without a glance in my direction and with what seemed like a heavy heart, she sighed and said:

"Time will tell, only time will tell."

My grandmother, on the other hand, responded to my questions on the prophecy with the opening lines from yet another hymn which made me a little more than just uncomfortable.

"I have decided to follow Jesus; I have decided to follow Jesus, no turning back, no turning back. The cross before me, the world behind me no turning back, no turning back."

"My child, in the old testament no one questioned the words of a prophet. Don't you be the first to do so."

Those were her last words on the subject. Even with my prodding, she refused to engage any further conversation on the subject.

Soon after the "prophecy" as everyone began to call it, a new family moved in next door to us with nine sons. My mother always wanted me to be a girly girl with frills, bows, and baby dolls. Somehow, that was not in my nature, so I resisted playing with dolls. I could not stand the gossip and pettiness of a bunch of girls. In fact, I managed to have only one real girlfriend throughout my entire school life. These boys next door were adventurous—they created objects, fixed things, and had big hopes and dreams for their lives. I was impressed and drawn to the adventure inherent in their actions. At first, I spent time watching from our window. Slowly, I was drawn to closer observation of what was taking place next door. They were noisy, to say the least. Creative, they nailed and hammered, made go-carts, wooden toys, miniature sailboats, and even spinning wheels. Their grandest effort in my opinion was the treehouse they built. I found myself asking questions. I also quickly learned when to be quiet in observation when I was around them. Before long, they began to draw me out of my shyness and I slowly but surely found that I could actually speak up for myself. They accepted me into the group as a tomboy and much later in life, I found out that they had all pledged not to desecrate the relationship in any way. I really came to believe that after a while, they did not see me as a girl at all. This allowed me to observe and learn a great deal about the mindset of the male species. As we grew up together, I was privy to watching them and even encourage them in their early attempts at engaging the attention of girls. It was with this newfound confidence that I met my first husband.

We were both teenagers. He was not a part of the group that I hung around. I first paid attention when he shared his ambition to leave our small country and travel to England to attend college there then see a piece of the world.

"You know anyone in England?" I asked really wanting an answer.

"No, don't know anyone there."

"Then tell me how you going to get a visa to go to England, you know you neeed a sponsor?"

"I don't know the answer to either of those questions"

Then placing his left hand at his heart, right hand raised to heaven he said forcefully.

"I don't know how yet, but so help me God I'm going to find/make a way to get to London."

This show of intention fired my imagination since I too longed to travel and see the outside world. The relationship started with a friendship, support, and encouragement for the dream he held in his heart. Growing up, I too was a dreamer and firmly believed in the statement "all things are possible if you believe." After listening to him fantazing about travel overseas I responded by saying:

"Close your eyes, take a deep breath, you're in London. What do you hear, what do you see behind your closed eyelids?"

There was a long pause with him standing there, eyes closed. Finally, he said with surprise in his voice.

"It's cold, very cold, my body is shivering. White stuff is falling out of the sky and my toes are frozen."

At the time, I did not have a name for what I had just asked him to do, but I did know that I would often close my eyes and see things that I wanted behind my closed eyelids. It was the very first visualization exercise that I had ever put someone through and it worked. When he finally arrived in London two years or so later, it was indeed snowing and he got frostbitten toes.

His family members could not see the possibility of a way out of the country; much less paying the way through college in a foreign country. The relationship started with a friendship around the desire we both had to get educated, travel, and see a bit of the world. You could well say that he had a dream to get out of then British Guinea and in a strong bond of friendship, we began to research and develop a plan to get him to England to be educated. It took two years of planning before we realized that we were in love. As was the custom of the time, he wrote a formal letter to my father asking to be considered as a suitor for my hand in marriage. My father disapproved of the match because, in his opinion, the extensive plans to go overseas were too sketchy; not to mention the fact that my father thought we were too young. He also prophesied and gave me a description of my "real" husband who he said resided in a foreign country that was not England. He told me that in all seriousness, he could not give my hand in marriage to anyone else. I was eighteen at the time and needed my father's permission and signature in order to acquire a marriage license. This conflict became the first and only time in my life that I ever challenged my father's judgment.

My mother, on the other hand, observed my determination and suspected that my rebellion could probably lead to elopement when I became of age. She, of course, wanted to have the joy of planning her only daughter's wedding and pleaded with my father who finally gave in. He agreed to signing the paperwork, paying for my wedding as was his responsibility, but refused to walk me up the aisle. When the British visa was acquired, we were married on a rainy day in January, weeks after my nineteenth birthday. It rained for three days prior to the wedding. As a bride, I was lifted in and out to the car and into the church because the streets around us were flooded. I entered the church in the pouring rain. My uncle walked me up the aisle; my mother and my aunt were ecstatic. When we left the church as husband and wife, the rain had stopped. The sun was shining upon the water in the streets —more speculation for the gossipers.

Our first son was born in Guyana eighteen months later much to the delight of his grandparents. There is also much tradition in our culture surrounding the birth of a baby particularly when it is a firstborn boy that opens the womb. My mother was present, supporting and praying throughout labor and delivery. Although I gave birth in a hospital, it was an elderly woman, a midwife, who delivered me. As soon as the mother and baby were cleaned up, my mother was allowed to enter the room. She and the midwife prayed over the baby and my mother performed the first ritual of my son's life. She took the newborn into her arms. Gently blowing the breath of Almighty God into the soft spot in the center of his head, to me, she said:

"Today, you have been blessed to become a mother. This boy child is the gift given to you by Almighty God."

"His father gave up the seed. You carried it in the womb. Your next task is to nurture, keep his spirit free; you will enjoy him for the period of time he is given to you."

I looked on with awe. I had never been privy to this ritual before.

"How?" I asked in bewilderment.

"Shhh, remember my daughter, this boy child does not belong to you. He is a child of God. He is loaned to you and your husband. If you do your job as a mother well, he will be raised to be a God-fearing, mannerly man who will have what it takes to attract to himself a woman of virtue, quality, and class."

"What does that mean?" I asked, tears streaming down my face.

"When the time comes and it will, you will turn him over to the woman who loves him as much as you do. You will always have the 'sacred' connection and the energy of the umbilical cord that you both carry within yourselves. It is a 'sacred' passageway that takes your prayers for him straight up to Almighty God."

Then, she sealed my son with the mark of the cross and a circle on his forehead and gently handed him back to me. This, in our culture, is called "the seal." It was the first and only child of five that my mother had the opportunity and privilege to "seal." The others were born in other countries. The last of which was born in the United States of America years after my mother had made her transition. With each succeeding child, I have used an adaptation of my mother's original blessing and seal.

CHAPTER FIVE

My baby boy enjoyed the blessing of our little family as well as the community around us. At four months old, he and I set out on the journey to join his father who was already in England. I arrived in London after a tedious three-week journey traveling first from Guyana by air to the Caribbean island of Trinidad in order to board a cruise ship to the United Kingdom. The journey was perilous as the ship got caught in a storm at the Bay of Biscay and I along with all the other passengers prayed for God to spare our lives. The first glimpses of England were not at all heartwarming; certainly not what was expected. The ship docked at Liverpool docks, which sits along the eastern side of the Mersey Estuary. It was the heart of winter, bitterly cold, damp, and unwelcoming. The landscape seemed dreary and for the first time in my life, I saw trees without foliage. Everything inside me yearned at that moment for the warmth of the tropics and the nurturing of a family. My husband had preceded us a few months before in order to get registered for college and find accommodation for the family. Both of our families were concerned that we had chosen to travel to a new land where there was no family support.

My only contact in England was a penpal; we had been writing to each other for just about a year. The high hopes with which the journey began were very quickly lowered by the dreary, unwelcoming atmosphere going through immigration and custom. It was, as it turned out, a journey with challenges for which we were most definitely not prepared. Moving from a warm tropical climate into the cold of England in the month of January was no fun. Unaccustomed to the weather and not equipped with proper winter attire, we were kept cold for all of the remainders of the winter. With no family in London to show us the ropes, discomfort and loneliness soon took hold of us. Caring for a baby in the heart of winter was extremely challenging. My husband who had been advised to learn a trade before he left Guyana soon found a job as a welder and started taking remedial math classes as soon as he arrived in London leaving me with long hours of loneliness. I was extremely shy. The Brits, of course, are not considered to be the friendliest nation on earth. With no one to talk to, I started to lose my voice frequently and became quite sickly.

Embracing the British customs, culture, and traditions proved to be challenging and required a great deal of patience to navigate. With time, we joined the Anglican Church on the corner, and Father Hugh and Betty his wife took us under their wings and into their family. Father Hugh, as he was fondly called by his parishioners, encouraged me to volunteer time in the church on weekdays while the church staff and other elderly volunteers took turns with the baby. At last, we began to experience the other side—the warmth of British culture. He afforded me the opportunity to develop some office skills and encouraged me to seek employment in the community. My very first job was working alongside very aggressive women on an assembly line in a frigid factory. The hours were long, conditions very rough, and if the truth be told, I was afraid of those women whose arguments often ended in physical altercations. Sometimes, their disputes caused them to be restrained and forcibly removed from the factory. This was the sixties and I had up until that time never heard cuss words streaming out of the mouths of women, but these women cursed with rhythm. We were a mixture of West Indian and white women doing "piece" work on a car assembly line. I hated the job—it was rough on my hands as well as my psychological well-being. Father Hugh in his wisdom encouraged me to hang in there long enough to be able to gain a good job-related reference. With the support of church members, the pastor, and his wife, I stuck it out for one full year. Soon, I was able to acquire a job at the British Railways Board as a clerk. With the passage of time, we moved from living in one room in a rooming house to better conditions sharing space of two rooms in the home of a church member. It was a family home and she and her twin boys became the first unit of family for us far away from home.

My husband at the time, truly motivated and determined to get an education, went to school full-time and worked part-time to take care of the family. His day often started at four-thirty in the morning and ended at around eleven at night. I felt like a single parent raising a child. We were both missing family, but being first of all shy and being a woman in a strange land, I felt the need for the company of people my own age who shared at least some of my cultural values. Eventually, it dawned on me that the seven men in my husband's study group, all from the West Indian Islands, may perhaps have girlfriends, wives, or family members in London. The hint worked to my advantage. I made contact and a surrogate family was soon developed. These women were all as lonely and afraid as I was. Soon, we discovered how much we needed each other, and before long, strong bonds of friendship grew into a unique family circle. We spent quality time together and shared information/ideas around survival in the deep freeze that was London. Mastering the art of dressing warmly in the frigid winter in London was a challenge for each and every one of us. Our parenting skills began to rub off on one another which benefitted me very much being the youngest in the circle. Most importantly, we created a unique kind of communal parenting where we pampered, disciplined, and cared for each other's children. We rotated babysitting at weekends; thus, creating time-out from parenting.

In the circle, we shared and respected each other's cultural backgrounds and faith. We became a deeply spiritual family in a foreign land seeking to live out the elements of our faith. What I did not recognize at the time was that I had organized my very first "sacred" woman's circle. We met in each other's homes at weekends. The "circle" became the place where we gathered weekly to laugh in the face of adversity, pray, play games together, and nurture ourselves. As women, we needed it for our men were heavily invested in study, school grades, and homework as well as working part-time to bring in what little money they could to keep the family going. Each week, a couple got the opportunity to step out leaving the kids within the safety of the rest of the family.

Immigrant life in London in the sixties was challenging enough without the addition of tragedy. Having a surrogate family was indeed the lifesaver and game changer that gave us the strength to keep going. We set our collective intention on graduation from college and into a life of progressive achievements. We were committed to reminding one another of those set ideals. Of the seven families in the group, Johnny, a family man in our community and his wife, stumbled under the weight of marital problems. The group encouraged him to cut back on his original stringent educational goals and he did. Under the weight of depression, however, he lost his way and his mind. Unfortunately, in a fit of anger, he took the life of his wife but survived his own suicide attempt. After he was taken into custody, the family clung together in grief. We wept and prayed for the "circle" to be strengthened as we clung together for the strength to stay the course and take care of the three children left behind. Johnny, who was a native of Guyana, was committed to a mental institution and eventually was deported to his native land. After he was gone, the group had to face the challenge of saying goodbye to the children as we put them on an airplane to return to their grandparents in Guyana. In those dark, dark days, the real challenge was to keep hope alive. I was the youngest in the group but as we prayed together, I found myself using my father's words to motivate and resuscitate the good intentions and goals we had set for ourselves.

"While we grieve for our brother and sister, let us not forget what it is that brought us together in this foreign land—the strive for education, the key that could lead us out of poverty, and our determination to make a better way for our children and grandchildren."

"Lest we forget," I would say, "we have to keep reminding ourselves and each other of our intentions every minute of each day."

It was a prayer that brought us through those grueling emotions and up against walls during the hardest times. Our basic survival was deeply rooted in the love and support that the church and our small community wrapped around us, and of course, raw, naked "faith." As a group, we loved one another and I have to acknowledge that our two white British neighbors were right there beside us silent, respectful, and faithfully locked in her own form of prayer on behalf of the group. There was no professional counseling or therapeutic intervention at our disposal; no social services to turn to in our hours of need. We checked on each other every morning and evening and created individual prayer partnerships one with the other to see us through the crisis. Later that same year, we lost another member—a sister from the circle—she died rather suddenly of acute kidney failure leaving her grieving husband and five children behind. The same technique we used in our earlier sessions was applied to the recurring emotions of deep grief. When one or two among us would ask "why" I would offer my grandmother's words as comfort.

"We don't question God," to which I would also add my father's words:

"He never said the road would be easy but rather, that he would never leave us."

Before the year was over, I was an up-close and a personal witness to the power of love and what it can accomplish. Our brother shook himself out of his grief to face the responsibility of raising children as a single parent with the support and love of our close-knit family. From this period of my life story, I got a hint that love overcomes tragedy. Two males in the remaining structure of our family found that the hardships of providing for family and staying on the roller coaster of life in the East End of London were too difficult, so they dropped out of school to better take care of the family. Three families made it through to graduation and turned their lives around enough to support the generation ahead of them.

CHAPTER SIX

It was a cold December day in London, my first day back at the office after a leave of absence of one month. We were expecting our second child—a pregnancy fraught with difficulty. I was in discomfort for most of the day. I glanced at the clock; it was 4:00 p.m. The pattern of the discomfort had shifted to that of labor pains. I was four months pregnant. I left the office early and got into the elevator. The only other person in the elevator was a beautiful young woman dressed in a Hindu saree. Much later, I learned that she was from Bombay, India. We rode in silence to the ground floor. The elevator stopped with a jerk as did elevators of that era and the pain in my stomach intensified. Beads of perspiration covered my brow and the young lady next to me asked in a concerned voice:

"Are you all right?"

"No," was my quick response.

She helped me out of the elevator toward the main door and hailed a cab. I gave the driver general directions to my home. My companion was so concerned for my safety she got into the cab with me.

"What's your name?" she inquired.

"I am Norma," I responded overcame by another wave of pain.

"My name is Celine and I think we should go to the emergency room."

Shaking my head forcefully with tears streaming down my face, I said:

"No, no, I got to pick up my son and get him home first."

"Don't think about that now. I am sure that will be taken care of, but first, we must get you medical help."

Another wave of pain hit me and I felt totally drained of my life's energy. Traffic in London during what we now call "rush hour" was painfully slow. The taxicab slowed to a halt in a traffic jam and the pain intensified; it was now almost unbearable. Soon, we were outside St. Bartholomew's hospital in London. The cab driver pulled into the emergency entrance. My companion with the help of the taxi driver helped me into the emergency room. I collapsed in the lobby and lost consciousness.

I regained consciousness to a hive of activity and excruciating pain. A young doctor, with urgency in his voice, explained to me that I needed surgery to remove the fetus that was dead in me. The pain was so intense that I begged the attendant doctor to just end it all by giving me a lethal injection. He was too focused on dealing with the emergency at hand to take me seriously or to address my request. However, a young Irish student nurse of twenty-years-old, who was just getting off duty overheard my request. She fell in a step alongside the moving trolly, took my hand, and speaking to me softly, exhorted me not to go into surgery in such a frame of mind. She was Catholic and she launched into *Hail Mary's*.

I remembered a needle in my arm, heavy fog. I'm not sure how long I blacked out but my next recognizable sensation was that of peacefulness. I found myself looking down on my body lying on the operating table surrounded by hospital staff. *I was baffled.* I could not comprehend how I could be looking down at the scene below while I was still lying on the table. *How can I be in two places at the same time?* I asked myself.

There was a strange feeling of being frantic at one level of consciousness, while at the same time, there was a sense of peace at another level. When I turned my awareness back to the medical emergency at hand, I wanted to assure the medical staff that there was really no need for the concern they displayed for my life. I was now fine, *I just needed*, I thought, *some answers about the two bodies.* Just then, the thought crossed my mind that I did not know how to get down from the ceiling. With the thought came mobility. I found myself standing on the ground amidst the medical staff. I looked on in shock as skillful hands worked to prepare me for surgery. When the surgeon picked up the instruments, I screamed at him that I was all right; he did not need to perform the operation nor did he have my permission to take my life. To my surprise, although I was up in his face, he seemed oblivious to my presence. I followed the nurses on their trips back and forth trying to get their attention but to no avail. They could not see or hear me. Suddenly, there was another hive of activity as the monitor indicated that I had "flatlined." I stared dumbly at the equipment. I knew what the position of the graph meant—I had flatlined. However, I could not believe it. When the doctor took the defibrillator in his hands, I could somehow see the outline of the corona of electricity and its intensity. My thoughts were very clear at this point, *I'm not dead. Somehow, there's a terrible mistake in this room. People are acting strange. Now the monitors are malfunctioning. I've got to get out of here before they actually take my life by mistake.*

In bewilderment, I found myself moving upwards out through the ceiling and into a very dark tunnel. There was the sensation of moving very swiftly through the tunnel. Suddenly, there appeared within the darkness a speck of welcoming light. As it pulsated and expanded, my eyes became riveted to the expanding field of light. Before I knew it, the end of the tunnel was before me with a burst of radiant, brilliant white light. As I drew closer to the light, I remembered thinking that if I survived the experience, I would probably be blinded by the brilliance of the light before me. I emerged from the tunnel into a crystal clear, radiant white light. There was a sense of merging. *There are no words to adequately describe the feeling of joy, radiance, and peace I experienced the moment I merged with the light. I became one with light and in so doing was acutely aware that I was also one with love.*

I remember wondering how one got around in this environment. As soon as the thought popped into my mind, I found myself moving swiftly toward a vast hallway with huge pillars. I was drawn to a massive screen. It lit up displaying three moving scrolls. I felt an incredible sense of peace and well-being. On the far lefthand side of the screen was my life scrolled in scenes the way it had been planned. Standing there, I *knew* that I had planned my life that way. Nothing I had read on earth had given me that information but at the moment, I *knew* it. The center column contained the life experiences I had during my twenty-six years of my life. On the far right hand side of the screen were the objectives of the experiences and what I should have learned from them. My head moved swiftly from one side of the screen to the other.

I noticed that the inscription at the end of each entry on the right hand side of the screen ended with the words "objective not accomplished." It was a compassionate assessment of my life as I had planned it as well as the way in which I had lived it. I was disappointed at having been so unaware of the nature of my life experiences and the blessings inherent in the situations and relationships represented in my life. During the review, I could see the places where I had prayed and the way in which each prayer had been answered. I was surprised to discover how unaware I was that the answers had shown up in my life. I also noted that no one had taken the time to teach me to be still and listen for the answer. It was clear that my prayers worked sometimes to my advantage; sometimes against me. The things I had asked God so often became obstacles in my way. From the record, I saw that some of these requests were counterproductive to the goals and objectives I had set for my life on earth. I asked the question at the record who taught me how to pray. I was shown the many people across lifetimes who had taught me the art and the skill. I previewed many scenes (The actual scenes that I previewed are the only part of the recollection of this experience that I've never been able to remember sequentially). There were scenes that related to my relationship with my parents. There were scenes from my life that seemed trifling when I lived them; now it was revealed to me the profound impact these had on my life. Try as I might over the years, I still cannot recall the actual sequence of the review.

The first scroll came to an end and I was acutely aware of the unfinished nature of my life—how ignorant I had been of the true meaning and purpose of my existence. I sensed a lack of accomplishment. The screen began to scroll again very slowly. This time, interwoven into the center screen, were scenes from other lifetimes that had a direct impact on the concepts I was expected to master in the life I had just left. I could see the repetition of experiences and the overlap from one lifetime to another—different people, change of surroundings, same lesson. I began to ask myself the question:

Why didn't somebody tell me there was more to life than meets the eye?

In response to this repetitive question, another recurring question popped into my mind:

What have you done with your life?

This question produced yet another scroll where I perceived scenes which I could easily have blamed parents or others for the outcome, but the question at the end of each scroll continued to be:

What have you done with your life?

It took months to get that recurring question out of my mind after I returned to earth. The screen blanked out and my attention again moved to mobility. With the thought, I found myself moving, still a part of the brilliant light, to a stream. Yes, for me there was a river, we sang about it all the time in church when I was a child.

"Yes we would gather at the river, the beautiful, the beautiful river, gather with the saints at the river that flows from the throne of God."

On the other side of the stream, there were hundreds of very happy people, all of whom I was very excited to see. I stopped at the edge of the stream and my aunt, who had recently died, stepped into the stream to greet me. Using what seemed like a net, she began to clear the moss on the surface of the stream. She attended to this task assiduously. Each time she managed to create a clear pathway on the surface of the stream, the two sections of moss would suddenly merge, nullifying her efforts. Finally, she looked up and addressing me directly, said:

"I am sorry, but you cannot cross now, you must return."

"Why?" was my disappointed response.

"Because you must go back. Tell them that there is more to life than meets the eye."

With the utterance of those words, I found myself falling rapidly as if from a great height, at great speed, and literally plunged consciously into my body. Excruciating pain hit my consciousness.

Finally, I awoke to emotional pain and a deep sense of loss. Over the next twenty-four hours, my body felt heavy, clammy, and disconnected from my spirit. I was very frustrated by the fact that I had no knowledge of how to consciously access the state of love and light that I had so recently experienced. My recuperation was slow; I wanted to return to the peaceful, blissful experience I had encountered beyond the tunnel. When I went home from the hospital, I discovered that my "spiritual sight" had been restored (As a child, I could see the aura around all living things. I had prayed and asked for this sight to be removed in order to cope with everyday living). I observed the hospital staff's chatter and could clearly see swirls of light surrounding their bodies. A few of them even had halos around their heads. I could also sense the chatter going on in their heads as they worked—schedules, personal insights, apprehension, and even their fancies and fears

The memory of this joyous state has been the fuel for my inner seeking and spiritual exploration. I am happy to tell you that I have in this physical body returned to the light three more times. I've found healing, loss of the fear of dying, uncovered much love/light, and found my purpose, and you can, too.

Upon my return to the reality that is life here on earth, I could not help but ask yet another question.

"Why," I questioned angrily, "had they sent me back?"

My question was met at first by a drone of silence which was eventually punctuated by the words of my departure from the other side.

"Tell them there is more to life than meets the eye."

Upon opening my eyes, taking my focus to my surroundings, I was aghast at discovering a range of new senses. Bright swirls of light surrounded the bodies of the hospital staff; it was a fascination to see color aligned to movement everywhere around me. I could sense the chatter going on in the heads of the staff on duty, schedules, personal information, personal fears, and apprehensions. It was a mind-altering shift of perspective.

Lunchtime each day was spent in the company of the Hindu lady. She visited every day while I was hospitalized. She patiently endured the deep silence. She did not want, as she put it, "to intrude on personal time with my husband" during the evening visiting hour, and so began one of the most deeply cherished friendships of my life that I honor and treasure to this day. A shy, simple, deeply devoted, praying Hindu woman, whose smile danced first in her eyes then moved to her lips; me a deeply devoted Christian woman fell in step together unaware that our world views and personal perspectives were about to change forever. We were strangers in a foreign land. Both of us are lonely but strong in our spiritual convictions/beliefs. It was a defining moment born out of a chance meeting that held deep empathy, sincere love, and care for one another. Neither of us, out of the love and respect we felt for each other, ever attempted to change one another's belief system. Later in the relationship, she shared her own story of loneliness and estrangement from family with only a brother and his family by her side. She was single and without children, unusual in her tradition for a female to be traveling in the world without a husband or family. Her silent prayerful presence was comforting in the midst of my deep grief for the loss of my baby; even more so, the pain and my grief of being separated from the divine light—the joy, peace, and completeness I'd experienced on the other side.

Lying in that hospital bed, I was trapped in a cold, clammy body that felt strangely foreign to me. The expansion of my five senses placed me squarely in a world of observation and wonderment. I could so clearly see swirls of light around the hospital staff as they performed their tasks. The effect of thoughts and language on the basic energy patterns of the body was truly intriguing. I was amazed at the *knowing* that came upon me. I seemed to *sense* quite naturally the state of health of some of the hospital staff around me and the major challenges in their lives. On the other side of that scale was my husband who seemed mystified by my deep introspection punctuated at odd times by unfathomable utterances that came out of my mouth.

"The lady in Room 413 is leaving us tonight."

I blurted out unexpectedly with a chuckle. The statement was not received very well by the staff who overheard me and seemed to know that I meant she was going to die.

"Hush, you are tired, just get some sleep."

The nurse would say, truly believing that I was hallucinating.

"Everything will be alright in the morning."

In the morning, the patient was dead. No, I was not tired. I was rejoicing at the fact that I *knew* that the patient was about to enter into the joy and bliss I had just oh-so-recently left behind me.

The actual near-death experience seemed so *sacred* to me I kept it to myself sharing it with no one—not Celine, the hospital staff, my pastor, nor even my husband. He observed me closely and expressed deep concern for the changes he observed in and around me. My perspective on life had changed and he worried about my mood swings. He questioned my doctors if there was a need for psychological evaluation and/or counseling. They referred me to my practitioner to answer his question. I left the hospital on a cold December day accompanied by my husband and my newfound friend *Celine.* For the next three years of my life, she became an integral part of our family. Exposed to the big, bright outdoors, my newfound senses became rather overwhelming. Swirls of light around the faces of the people going by intrigued me. My life in the spiritual fast lane with heightened senses had begun and I was not at all ready or prepared to deal with it. A constant stream of rhythm and music flowed through my brain constantly. I could sense its construction and understood its synchronization.

Three years of depression followed my release from the hospital brought on by my inability to cope with the new reality and conscious awakening. I instinctively knew that some kind of "shift" had taken place; however, at the time, I had no words to express or describe my feelings and/or processing. I reasoned that it may have been a shift in "consciousness"—a word that popped into my mind and stayed there for a long time before I understood its meaning. It was soon made clear to me that this new way of being was permanent. I could now see, sense, and feel things even before they happened. Electronic equipment around me seemed to malfunction in my presence often embarrassingly so. I'd walk under street lamps that would flicker and turn themselves off when I approached. Clocks and watches around me ran way ahead of time. To this day, I do not wear watches because, invariably, they carry the wrong time. However, it was a new understanding of music and energy that took my breath away. Growing up as a child, music was all around me— church and popular music streaming from the radio; there was even a cousin who sang with a jazz band and I was privy to their rehearsals. In my new reality with eyes closed, listening to music I could see colorful, well-integrated streams of energy weaving through the notes and the presence of light. I saw in my mind's eye the intricate shapes and patterns created by music—the amazing way in which the notes and patterns impacted the human energy field. Following the patterns with my mind's eye, I saw that each note tied to a color, every color linked to a number, and every number to a mathematical symbol. I was, and still am, fascinated by the interaction of energy in and around all living things. I began to feel disconnected from the everyday world of fantasy and denial and suicidal thoughts began to surface. I was looking for a way out of the turmoil and stress that filled my waking hours. It was at this point that I began to plan my exit. I tried stepping into heavy traffic but miraculously escaped with my life and that brought bitter disappointment. Next, I thought I would make an even more determined effort. I was careful to ask a friend who was an emergency nurse the exact amount of pills to take to end my life. Armed with the information, I acquired what I needed, cleaned the house, showered, dressed my young son, and sent him out to play in the backyard. Standing in the bathroom, a glass of water in one hand, pills in the palm of the other hand, I said what I thought would be my last prayer. My focus was penetrated by the voice of my son yelling at the top of his voice.

"Mommy, mommy," he shouted running through the house.

Finally, he finds me frozen over the bathroom, ready to swallow the pills in my hand. Oblivious to the scene before him, he opened up his little hand to disclose the source of his excitement.

"Look what I found Mommy."

He took over the moment, his eyes twinkling with the delight of his discovery.

"Half a butterfly, half worm, look Mommy!"

I immediately heard the whisper of a soft, little voice in my ear. *And who will explain the wonders of the world when you are gone?*

An unexplainable calm spread over me. I turned the palm with the pills over and dropped them into the toilet bowl. I emptied the contents of the glass of water, picked my son up, and hugged him tightly as I re-experienced the wonder of the gift that he was in our lives. The next logical thought in my mind was that if I tried to re-enter the world on the other side by way of suicide, *they* may very well send me back again to earth. This was something that had not crossed my mind before. Holding my son closely to my heart, I found myself thinking aloud:

"Perhaps there is a way to return even if only for just one short visit."

We left the house together, hand in hand; my little baby boy unaware that he had just saved his mother's life. We walked to the playground with me reveling in the joy of my son's excitement. I watched with renewed interest as he engaged in joyful play—climbing the monkey bars digging away in the sandpit. For the first time since my return from the other side, I found some peace in the idea of trying to find a way to make even a short, temporary visit back to the other side. Seventeen years before Raymond Moody introduced to the the world the term "near-death experience," I eventually gave up hope of finding an explanation for what had happened to me. My attention was now turned to finding a way back to the light that I knew to be very real. I vowed before God that I would find an acceptable way back to the light and this became not only just a desire within me but the purposeful intention of my life. On that fateful day, the journey to uncover the answer to the question "Who are you?" began. The search to *know* my spiritual *identity*, to *claim* my birthright, and to live out my desired purpose were all etched into my heartbeat. Even though at that time I had never heard the phrase "the power of intention," I was destined to have a living experience. The next saying that dropped in my head was the ancient saying:

"Get the body fit; the mind will follow."

I instinctively threw myself wholeheartedly into exercise, stretching, yoga, walking, and the whole rhythm of my life began to change for the better.

My husband by this time was now convinced that there was something really wrong with me. He is at a loss to truly understand the shift in personality as well as the intense discipline and routine that he observed in me. He tried to convince me that I need to see not just a psychologist but rather a psychotherapist. Every nerve within me was diametrically opposed to the idea and I said it forcefully.

Communication between us became very strained. My new-enhanced level of perception told me that my husband had a secret life outside of the marriage. However, I was not at all ready to accept nor was I strong enough to investigate the matter. I threw myself into my new routine of exercise, yoga, and quiet contemplation down by the water's edge close to where we lived. Also, I found myself spending as much time as I could spare visiting the beautiful chapel of the Episcopal Church where we worshipped. Here I would catch swirls of light streaming through the stained glass windows. It was where I first caught a glimpse of the majesty and beauty of an archangel in all its glory. I was sitting quietly alone in the back of the church one weekday when Father Hugh entered the sanctuary and lit the first candle. He dropped to his knees silently and for some unknown reason, rose and lit two additional candles on the altar. When the third candle sprang to life, the archangel appeared and I gasped aloud at the beauty and splendor of the magnificent image before my eyes.

"What is it, my child?" Father Hugh turned around and asked anxiously.

"What are you seeing? Tell me what it is that you see."

My eyes were transfixed upon the amazingly beautiful image before my eyes.

"It's an *angel*," I whispered, then quickly corrected myself:

"No, it's an angel with huge wings. It's an archangel."

"In the name of the Father, the Son, and to the Holy Ghost," Father uttered the words as he made the sign of the cross.

I slid off the pew and onto my knees, head bowed in reverence to the glory and majesty of what was before my eyes. It turned out that Father Hugh firmly believed in angels and I had given him his first real-life description of the image of an archangel. Our love of angels drew the two families closer together. He taught me much about the hierarchy of heaven, the angelic realms, and divine intervention. Father Hugh, as he was fondly called by his parishioners, was indeed a man of God. He taught me much about spiritual discipline, order, and sacredness. He was the second person in my life to prophesy my *call* to the ministry. Later, he mourned the fact that because I was a female, he could not recommend me for ordination and vows in the Episcopal church. His wife Betty felt the same way. She was a lovely woman, kind, and compassionate with a keen sense of humor and gifted hands. An avid gardener, parishioners would bring their half-dead plants to her and she would lovingly nurse them back to life. She also had a gentle soothing effect on young children which was so beautiful to observe. Everything she touched seemed to blossom, she loved nature and introduced me to the joys of an English garden.

"Be mindful," she would say.

"When you remove a plant or sapling from its natural setting in nature to place it indoors, you have chosen to become for the plant what God is to you—provider, sustainer, and protector."

"How so?" I asked wide-eyed.

"You choose to become caretaker of its very existence. Be as kind and caring to the plant as God is to you."

Her ability to love and her compassion touched me very deeply and we developed a beautiful mother-daughter relationship that supported me to try for the baby girl I so wanted.

CHAPTER SEVEN

My fourth pregnancy brought a wealth of medical problems. I was in my first trimester when I developed German measles. After careful medical examination, my doctors recommended an abortion based on the premise of possible birth defects and the state of my own health. That small voice in my head told me that despite the medical evaluation and subsequent report everything was going to be alright. I defied the doctors and ignored the advice from two members of mythe community who were registered nurses in a London hospital. The medical profession in London was not happy with my resistance to their advice. I was cautioned that if I went into spontaneous advance labor, the doctors would do nothing to save the pregnancy. I was at least in agreement with the doctors on this ruling. Hospitalized with high blood pressure, I spontaneously went into labor. Labor pains plagued me throughout the night but stopped suddenly in the early hours of the morning. My doctors placed me on complete bed rest. The extended family and my neighbors took turns to take care of my household and the two boys. They visited me in hospital and kept me informed of their progress. Earth angels, black and white, as I referred to them, diligently at work in the life of my family in our time of need.

Long hours of rest and quiet opened up my sixth sense and I became acutely aware that all was not well with my family back in Guyana. I sensed that my husband was withholding a letter from home and I kept on asking about it. He eventuall consulted with the extended family who supported him in breaking the news to me of my mother's sicknes. He shared the letter he received from from my aunt announcing my mother's cancer diagnosis and hospitalization.

The prognosis was not at all good and I was besides myself with worry. In our tradition, daughters are the ones who take care of ailing mothers and I was my mother's only daughter. Once again, Celine, my Hindu earth angel, was at my bedside to comfort and bring much-needed tranquility at a time of intense distress and worry.

"Just breathe," she would say with that special twinkle in her eyes.

"Your God will make a way."

"Let it be, just let it be, there's a way out."

She would say these words in such a sweet, comforting voice that I began to believe her. She had a way of turning her head to one side so she could wink at me which always made me smile. At home, the "circle" of an extended family kept my household and my two boys going in my absence. My husband, on the other hand, now had to add hospital visits to his already overcrowded schedule. By now, my extended family had expanded to include two of my white, blue-eyed British neighbors, and my Hindu *soul sister*. Adversity was teaching me the true meaning of words such as "collaboration," love, and "extended family."

I wanted to be at my mother's side as soon as I received the news of her diagnosis. However, ahead of me lay the task of a safe delivery of our third child before any other plans could be put in place. Transplanting our family from London back to the homeland was a big decision to make. It required in-depth rounds of discussions and decision making. At first, there was disagreement between us as a married couple surrounding the wisdom of breaking down the comfortable life we had struggled so hard to build in London in order to move back home. We had waded through the struggles of life in a strange country with my nuclear family oceans away. I was aware that I was asking God to grant me one miracle that my baby would be healthy—and another to grant me a way back home to be with my mother in her time of need. Was this too much to ask of God? Selena's words however, stayed with me night and day as I prayed.

"Talk to your God and then just let it be!"

The confidence she exuded as she said these words comforted me and gave me hope. We may not have been praying to the same

God is what I believed at the time, but she encouraged me to put faith in the God I served.

"He knows what you are feeling, what you are going through, he won't let you down."

I humbled myself before God and beseeched his guidance.

"What shall I do, Lord?" I asked over and over again lying in that hospital bed.

"Show me, guide me," I pleaded.

"What steps should I take?"

In the desert of uncertainty, God answered my prayer and made a way. The solution to the problem had to have been sent from above. My husband, considering the move and what it would cost to return home and resettle, was hesitant and perhaps rightly so. At the last moment, without a request from us, a letter arrived from our embassy inviting my husband to return to Guyana under a repatriation plan. God had answered my prayer and I was delivered of a healthy, baby girl. As soon as I was released from the hospital, we turned our affairs over into the hands of a well-respected lawyer and began the preparation for our return back to the motherland.

We made the move from England to Guyana when our daughter was one-month-old. A group of faithful people worked tirelessly to sort, pack, and make us ready for the move. Celine, in the meantime, was also in the throes of resettlement to Australia. On reflection, life in England had its difficulty, its lessons, and its joys. I walked away with many lessons gleaned from challenges too many to mention here. Among the lessons learned was rooted in my real-life "good Samaritan" Celine. Another lesson never to be forgotten—the value of love and the comfort of family. The recognition of the value of "family" is so important that in the absence of day-to-day access to the nuclear family, the universe or God if you will, provides a surrogate family. Ours was born of seven West Indian families that soon expanded to include two blue-eyed, blond British neighbors, and an Asian family. We laughed, cried, struggled, made plans for our lives, and supported each other's dreams. In a strange, peculiar way, we kept hope alive in each other's lives even in the midst of despair. On the day of our departure from London, the final goodbyes at Heathrow Airport were gut-wrenching. There was gratitude on both sides of the spiritual "family" to what I termed as the "earth angels" who had so lovingly supported us as well as friends and well-wishers who kept us going with love and kindness beyond measure.

Family reunions bring so much love and joy. At the other end of the journey home, the air was filled with festivities and excitement as we landed back on Guyana's soil. My two boys and the new baby girl were introduced to the family they did not know. The boys were both moved by the number of family members at the airport who greeted us with excitement. They were smothered and overwhelmed by the feelings of love and acceptance they experienced. I was surprised to see how frail my mother had become. Twelve years of separation spanned by miles of distance, longing, and sometimes despair had taken its toll. I set about taking charge of my mother's recovery from surgery, resettling my household, and adjusting the family to the culture shock of living in a third world country. Within months of our return, before I had a real chance to engage my father in discussions of spiritual matters, he died rather suddenly of a heart attack. Family and the entire community mourned his passing including former students whose lives had been dramatically changed by his influence. At the repast, many of these former students and members of the community gave testimonies to what my father had done in their lives. There were people who testified to healings they experienced at my father's hands. We knew that there was a spiritual side to him but certainly not about the healing. For me, it was all very overwhelming not only to hear but also to *feel* the depth of the grief of these people who were strangers to me. I heard these people say that they were all asked by my father not to speak of these things while he was alive. In thinking about it now, it did indeed sound like the Biblical "tower of Babel" as they all talked over each other. While experiencing my grief I was drawn to something he would often say to me.

"You are the eldest. Whatever you choose to do with your life, I expect you to produce seven times more than I ever could."

"Why?" I would ask perplexed by the statement.

"Because," he would say with emphasis.

"Your world, the one you will grow to maturity in, will offer you far more opportunities than I could ever have in mine."

Needless to say, standing in the moment, in the midst of overpowering testimonies around me, I was not only humbled but doubtful of how much I could achieve.

In his last note to me, there were seven pieces of instructions— one of which was "No flowers at the funeral." My father loved fresh flowers; everyone who knew him was aware of that. So, to everyone, it seemed a very strange request, but I understood his reasoning. He did not want poor people to spend precious money on flowers for his funeral or, for that matter, local gardeners who made a living from the sale of flowers, people he knew well, to give up blooms that kept food on the table for their families. Despite this request, on the day of his funeral at the graveside, there was a mountain, and I mean a mountain of fresh flowers. Here was a community saying goodbye to a respected voice in their lives—one who had taught/motivated their children and nourished their lives at many levels. I understood that they needed a tangible way, even a form of sacrifice on their part, to express their feelings and they did. The shock of his passing weakened my mother who, on her return home from my father's funeral, voiced these sentiments:

"I just buried the only man I have ever loved. My children are grown, I want to go join him on the other side."

At the time I attributed this statement to grief on her part and the effects of the shock of my father's sudden passing, I myself was inconsolable so I turned inward and locked everyone out including my husband. I was struggling to be strong for my mother. I read to her and kept the house full of beautiful music; particularly music that she and my father enjoyed. Sharing my experiences, she was the very first person to hear excerpts from my near-death experience shared with the backdrop of beautiful, relaxing jazz. My youngest brother who was sixteen years of age at the time became a part of our household.

The timing of my mother's passing eighteen months later was foretold to me in a dream weeks before she made the transition. In the dream, I was happy to know that she would experience the love and light that had been my own temporary passing over. Upon awakening, however, I was conflicted by grief that overcame me whenever I thought of living with the absence of her physical presence in my life. Soon after the dream, I was sitting listening to an intricate piece of drumming music when a miniature version of my father materialized in our fish tank in the living room.

"Where are you?" I asked excited and surprised at the same time by the image.

"No time to answer that."

He responded so clearly that I could hear the words in my head.

"But you look so well."

"There's very little time. Imagine that a match has been struck and all the time that I have with you is how long it takes for the light of the match to burn out. Listen carefully."

"Do you remember your recent dream?"

"Yes, I do," I responded rather excitedly.

"Listen carefully. After the event takes place, you know what I mean, you will clean the space and light candles to light up the way through the tunnel."

"Let your mother know all is well. I will be there to greet her on the other side."

"I will," was my nervous response to this peculiar request.

The tape I was listening to then moved to a jazz version of Mozart's 40th Symphony in G minor. The image in the tank quickly merged into yet another miniature version of my father; only this time, he was a maestro in tucks, tails, and top hat. He raised the baton in his hand gracefully and conducted the symphony. I was indeed delighted. This was a confirming sign. During his lifetime, I had often teased him that he had missed his true calling as that of a conductor of classical music. He had come back to let me know that my mother's passing over was imminent and to ask that I give her a message. In return, he afforded me the joy of watching him conduct one of his favorite pieces of music.

"Let her know that I will be there waiting on the other side."

And just like that, in the twinkling of an eye, his image faded before my very eyes.

Days after this experience, my mother's condition worsened. Her compassion and empathy shone through right to the end. On the morning before her passing, she insisted that I take her to the local hospital knowing that she would be admitted. We had put private care in place at our home supported by weekly doctor visits because third world hospitals in the sixties and seventies left a lot to be desired. Her request baffled me; when pressed for a reason, she responded in a way that was so typical of my mother:

"I don't want my grandchildren to feel afraid when they enter this room after I am gone."

During the wee small hours of the night, she had indicated to me that she was ready to leave and I was still processing this with deep sadness.

"I want them to remember the joyous times we shared in this space."

The tears I had been holding back for so long gushed out of me like a river. It took hard work to stay positive, especially in my mother's presence. We had talked about so many of her memories and before I knew it, I was sharing with her the joy I experienced crossing over to the other side. She was keenly interested and asked questions. I wanted more than anything else for her to be comfortable and at peace at her passing.

"My daughter," she whispered.

"Dry your eyes. All my life I have served and praised God. I'm going home to meet him, give thanks and praises. There is no need for tears."

"Call your brother in America, tell him I love him, let him know that he does not have to come home for the funeral."

We watched her, my youngest brother, husband, and I, for six hours on that Saturday morning. At noon, she uttered her very last words:

"The stone which the builder rejects shall become the head cornerstone."

And with those words on her lips, she drew her last breath to journey through the tunnel and into the light.

In the days and long nights of mourning, I turned those words over and over in my mind. Oddly enough, the meaning behind those last words escaped me for a very long time. Today, I understand. I am now the only living ordained clergy in two generations of pastors. I've taken the mantel of shepherd into prisons. Given the circumstances of my birth experience and rejection by the church, those words are clear and now understandable. Today, it is not only well with my life; it is well with my soul.

Despite my beautiful near-death experience and the knowledge that life on the other side is indeed glorious, I grieved the passing of my parents, felt deserted, and identified myself as an orphan for a very long time. In my grief, I became very private, refused to let anyone in, and subsequently became increasingly aloof and more introspective. My father had left me a list of seven spiritual books and I threw myself into reading. I was here reading a book by a Buddhist author that I stumbled upon the term the "Akashic Record" and for the first time could put a name to the record I had reviewed in my near-death experience. I was fascinated by the Buddhist concept of walking the middle way; it resonated well with me. When friends began to worry that I was becoming a loner and encouraged me to let people back into my life, I listened and soon got very involved in community development. My children, the true joys of my life, became my only comfort. Being the wife of a successful man in a third world country with all of its status and social benefits was no longer sufficient nor satisfying to me. Questions about my true identity and my life's purpose occupied my mind constantly along with a persistent, baffling question "what's next?" In the meantime, my marriage was on the rocks. I made the startling discovery that my husband and I had begun the journey of drifting apart. Upon reflection, I soon realized that silently and unknowingly, our marriage relationship was held together by a series of *projects* and the welfare of the children— projects such as acquiring education in a foreign country, survival, the struggle to fit into British life, homeownership, and finally, the remigration back to our homeland were all major contributors to the survival of the marriage. But now, I could sense from his actions that my husband seemed to have established for himself a private life outside of the marriage. It's not that we argued a lot; we just fell into extreme politeness. Communication was strained, more often than not, sadly lacking. However, since we had servants working inside of our home, the atmosphere was kept sterile and grievances were kept so private that we would leave the house to argue.

Growing into my new world perspective made me restless since I had not chosen to speak openly or publicly to anyone about my near-death-experience and my new perspective, my behavior seemed baffling to most people around me. To my husband, it was becoming an increasing cause for concern. His perspective led him to believe that I needed psychological intervention. He constantly urged me to seek out psychological help. The only person with whom I had shared my *sacred* experience was my dying mother. After she left the world, I was acutely aware that she had taken the secret with her to the grave and hoped that it would stay there so there was no one to talk to about the monumental changes taking place in my life. From my husband's observation of the changing patterns in my life, he began to voice his suspicions that I may be losing my mind. However, within me the ordinary five senses had expanded and I could see, react to, and commune with spirits from the other side. While I was super careful not to reveal the extent of these new senses, occasionally, I found that things I would say that relate to the other side would slip out and cause unexplainable awkward moments. My husband, struggling with the application of logic to understand my mood swings and personality changes, continued his advocacy for psychological intervention. Every nerve in my being resisted this path. He was openly resistant to the changes he observed within me; my silence about the near-death experience did not help the situation either.

One of the places where the change in me was most evident was in the music I listened to and played around the house. There was not just a shift but rather a real change in my record and music collection—serious jazz, Miles Davis, Coltrane, well-structured rhythms, and a new collection of what I termed "visionary" music— Neil Diamond's music and particularly his lyrics. His lyrics reached deep inside of me and stirred my very soul. One example of a deeply defining moment for me was the evening of a very special social occasion in our home—a cocktail and dinner party organized for a list of socialites. The servants worked diligently to set the perfect backdrop for the event. Standing in the living room waiting to receive my guests wearing a beautiful evening dress, well-coiffured, and ready for a social evening of fun. It dawned on me that receiving guests was not at all what I wanted to do. Looking around me, the beauty of the floral arrangements stood out. However, in the midst of the ambiance of the moment, there was this feeling of loneliness that stayed with me day in and day out. It was an emptiness, a space that the things and trappings of the world could not fill. For the first time in my life, the emptiness of the world of fashion, glamor, and social engagement actually seemed unnatural. Standing in the moment, I wanted to escape going through the motions of empty chatter. Reaching out for music to fill the gap, Neil Diamond's *I Am* was conveniently placed on the turntable. Hitting the on button, the words screamed at me "I am, I said . . . To no one there and no one heard at all, not even the chair." Time itself seemed to stand still as I listened with an acute awareness. These words screamed at me and jolted me wide awake although I was not sure exactly where my consciousness was in that moment. My life had become "the story of the frog who dreamed of being a king and then became one." Greeting the arriving guests seemed strangely odd in the midst of laughter, fun, and what seemed like idle chatter. I felt the loneliest I had ever felt in my life. The recurring question in my head throughout that evening was:

Who am I? What have I become?

Instead of an answer, there was just an empty void inside. We had worked hard to earn the social status we enjoyed. Every prayer we had offered up to God had been answered with more than we had asked for. Our lives represented to everyone looking in a huge success. Yes, like the lyrics in the song, I felt trapped between two shores— Guyana my native home to which we had returned but could not really fit in; England where we had lived for twelve years but which was most definitely not home. The new perspective brought on by the near-death experience had taken me through a paradigm shift. I was more emphatic; so much about people, who they really were, evolving beings of light, was now wide open to me. Yes, we had come in from the cold of London but sadly, the sum total of my new, enhanced senses brought me to a yearning and deep emptiness.

With the responsibilities of my mother's upkeep and well-being gone, the search for truth and for a way back to the light was now a priority. An ever-growing reading list now sat on my bedside table that included exploring the Buddhist philosophy. There I learned that my near-death experience had indeed taken me to review the file of my life at the Akashic record. My Christian beliefs had not provided me with information on the existence of such a record. Although impressed with a rather simple Buddhist concept—walking the "middle way"—I never felt the need to give up my Christian belief or its traditions. Meditation appealed to me and it became an active part of my daily routine. It resonated with me through the Bible verse – "Be still and know that I am God." Meditation placed me in a space of calm and serenity that brought comfort to my restless spirit. To relieve boredom, I took a teaching position in a two-year college. My preparation for facing a class of young people with their auras arrayed before my eyes began with meditation, stretching and relaxation. Standing before a typical class of thirty or so students with a multitude of auras before me as clear as crystal, it was necessary to remember that my task in this forum was not to clear chakras and auras but rather to motivate students, particularly girls to be excited about learning. My father's favorite words, the one-liner repeated over and over again often came to my rescue:

"Education is the key."

A few of my own choice words were sometimes added to that statement. I had become a role-model for young people in a third world country who longed to spread their wings and set themselves free.

Deep breathing exercises were also very helpful to release the not-so-positive energy that could be felt in the classroom environment. I threw myself into community development, bringing information and help to those who were poor and marginalized. At this stage of my life, creative writing became appealing and I wrote an award-winning play. Writing provided a way of expression and communication within me that was free and clear. In a way, it also provided a platform from where the ongoing desperate search could continue.

"Who am I?"

"Why can't I remember the details of all the past lives I have lived?"

"Is there a real pathway to finding spiritual truth?"

My Christian religion gave me faith and reminded me constantly of the rich stories from the scriptures. However, it failed to truly lead, nourish, or guide me to the depth of living the word day by day. Now that I found myself fully awake, there was a desire to know how to walk the spiritual talk, how to heal the sick, and how to feed some of the spiritual information that now flooded my mind into those who needed to be awakened. So many questions yet so hard to find the answers rooted, grounded in real true-to-life spiritual day-to-day habits. Where and how does one begin such a search? Little did I know that the means of finding the answers was about to present itself. The teacher as well as some of the answers soon surfaced out of the ashes of my late father's words:

"When the student is ready; the teacher will appear."

Persistence in asking my father deep questions produced this response over and over again.

"How does one recognize the teacher?"

This repeated answer brought frustration.

"Live long enough," he would say, "and you will come to know that experience does teach wisdom. Believe me when I say that you will recognize wisdom when it appears on the horizon of your life."

With a sigh, I would think but refrain from voicing the sentiment.

"Spoken like a true English teacher."

Years later, these words kept surfacing in the middle of my efforts at serious meditation. I was seeking clear answers to the questions that plagued my waking hours. It was on my walks in nature that I began to feel and express my readiness for the answers. On one of those long walks, the memory crept into my mind that Christ spoke in parables for a reason. So I resigned myself to waiting patiently for the answer. When I least expected it, what do you know, the teacher did in fact show up quite unceremonially. After reviewing several referrals, my husband and I set out to interview a prospective applicant for the task of clearing the land we had bought for the purpose of building our family home in Guyana. "Brother" as everyone called him had come with very good references and stories that spoke quite highly of his competence, experience, and integrity. The meeting was scheduled to take place at the proposed building site. When we pulled up, two men, an older man and a young man were already at the site awaiting our arrival. I got this strange, perplexing feeling that

I had somehow lived through this moment before. However, as the meeting progressed, an old Guyanese saying kept popping into my head—"There is more here than meets the eye"—and, sure enough, I was totally unprepared for what lay ahead. This perception quickly proved to be true. In my spirit, I felt sure that the encounter was a lot more than just clearing physical space for construction.

Patiently awaiting us were two men. A tall young man, knees bent, and seemingly rather impatient squatted in the shade of a large tree. The older of the two men, I estimated as perhaps in his late sixties to early seventies stood erect, patiently waiting in the shade of another tree. As I observed him, there was a distinct sense of peace and tranquility around his aura field. This caught my attention as well as my curiosity. He was medium height, about five-seven, rather muscular without an ounce of body fat. Grey dreadlocks crowned his face and reached down to the center of his back. His face glowed with an abundance of white light. I could see distinct lines of serenity and authority in his energy field; something I had not quite seen so profoundly outlined in the energy field of any other human being. I was intrigued, to say the least. The car pulled up, both men moved forward to greet us; the older of the two in the lead. As my husband stepped from the jeep he was driving, it was the older of the two that spoke first; his hands respectfully crossed behind his back.

"Good maning Sir."

"Good morning to you, too."

"I am Brother, that's what everybody call me."

The two men shook hands while I remained in silent observation in the car. I scrutinized their faces and body language carefully and found it to be a rather pleasant or better still, exhilarating mix of energy.

"This is my grandson, Arthur," the old man said proudly, "everybody call him Art."

"He's one of two grandchildren that gonna work with me to get this job here done."

He smiled and the warmth of his smile was beautifully reflected in the radiance and resonance of his aura.

"Get you ready for building in no time, Sir."

"Glad to meet you, and even happier to hear that," was my husband's smiling response.

"They tell me you're the man for the job, have you done work like this before?"

"Yes, Sir, the Miller house, Laweyr Fields right next to you here, and a lot of others. I'm the man they call when they need to clear space one way or another."

"Good to know, so here we are, let's take a look at the layout of the land."

The three men fell in step and in conversation together moving along a steep pathway and out of my earshot. Here and there, they stopped occasionally to point out what seemed to be landmarks along the way. It was, however, the persona and the light around the older man that held my attention even at a distance. He was very respectful, purposeful in his stride, and ready, it seemed, for the task at hand. I could not put my finger exactly on the reason why I *felt* that this old man was wise beyond measure. I was intrigued by the light in his eyes which was also reflected in the glory of his aura. Even in his humble state, he walked with a full stride of authority, dignity, and purpose. After what seemed like a long conversation, the three men scrutinized blueprints and plans, shook hands over what seemed like a verbal agreement, and strolled back to the truck in a lighthearted conversation about the weather.

"Let me introduce you to my wife," my husband said pointing to me sitting in the truck.

"Very good to meet you, ma'am," the old man said.

He tipped his tattered hat and accompanied it with a courteous bow. We did not shake hands; his remained crossed behind his back. The younger man met my eyes, he followed his grandfather's gesture, and tipped his hat but held his silence. Two days later, when the work started, I drove to the site alone to get a sense of the team that was created to accomplish the arduous task of clearing and breaking ground for construction. I expected to see perhaps four to six men supervised by Brother. To my surprise, it was Brother and his two grandsons. Brother's shirt was paced to his skin with sweat indicating that he was working as hard as the two younger men. It was around noontime, lunchtime for the crew. As I approached, I saw the old man refreshing himself at the waterhole they had created. He walked over to sit under the shade of a tree. Initially, he seemed to ignore my presence which made me feel that I was being intrusive on the crew's lunch hour. I watched from the car as he washed and dried his hands, then reaching for what seemed like a homemade bag, pulled out a large Bible. He kissed the cover and carefully placed the Bible on a stand and then proceeded to uncover his homemade lunch. The group of two other men worked strenuously clearing undergrowth. It seemed they had designated staggered lunchtimes. I watched from a distance observing with a keen interest the reverence of the moment.

Soon, I was paying routine daily visits to the site. One peculiar thing caught my attention—there was always a large Bible in close proximity to the old man whenever he ate lunch. Rumors from the community and my house servants had indicated to me that Brother was respected by the community as a "wisdom keeper" on the planet. So on my third visit, I broke my usual silent observation and initiated a conversation by asking about the ever-present Bible.

"You take your Bible everywhere you go?" I asked cautiously.

"Yeah, why? You find something wrong with that?"

The question was sort of thrown out there casually. I did not think that he would be bothered by my answer one way or another.

"No, no, not at all," was my quick response.

"It's just, well . . ." I stammered and stopped abruptly.

"Out with it. Don't ever hold back what's on the tip of your tongue, my child."

"Well, everyone says you're a 'wisdom keeper' so I figured there's a lot of information running around in your head."

The old man chuckled; he seemed really amused by the statement.

"This book here, the Bible, to my knowledge, is where to find wisdom. I asked God to grant me lil bit of that wisdom, put it into my heart, who knows, because I keep the book around me, he may just have done that, may just have done that my child."

"I never thought of it like that," I said rather surprised.

"You could be quite right."

"Do you read the Bible?" he inquired of me.

"Yes, I do, although not too sure I understand it all. I have many questions."

"You do? Hmm."

I surveyed his face trying to make up my mind about posing one of those questions that intrigued me. A sixth sense told me that he was open to receiving the question.

"In the Bible, where did the women come from that became wives to Adam's sons?"

He threw his head back and laughed heartily. The laughter puzzled me and made me feel a little foolish for having asked a question this wise man did not seem to take seriously in the first place, but I did want an answer.

"That's your burning question?" he asked with amusement.

"I can see . . ."

I found myself stumbling over the next set of words.

"That you find my question amusing. For me, it's a very serious question. I've been seeking the answer to this question since I was about eight or nine. No one has even tried to answer it."

"Who you been asking?"

"People in Bible study, pastors, people who should know the answer."

He turned his head to one side as he stroked his beard, his eyes never leaving my face.

"Now I'm asking you and . . . waiting for an answer."

"Can I ask what is your first name?"

"Norma."

"Do you know what it means?"

"They tell me, the teacher."

"And they are right."

"I don't feel like a teacher, there is so much that baffles me, so much I do not understand and very little that I know."

"Do you know who named you?"

"My father," I responded, feeling suddenly rather serious.

"An old soul, he knows a thing or two."

"How do you know that?"

He shrugged his shoulders avoiding the question. Curiosity was now getting the better of me. The look on his face suggested to me that he was re-evaluating his first impressions of me.

I also made a mental note that he used the present rather than the past tense when he referred to my father. My father had already crossed over to the other side. His choice of words told me that the old man was aware of the fact that the spirit lives on forever. However, I was still expecting an answer to my question.

"Well? Is there an answer to my question?"

I asked with my eyes riveted to his face trying to determine if he did have an answer and, if so was he prepared to share it? I was growing impatient.

"Do you know where the woman in the Bible called 'Eve' came from?" he asked.

"The book says, 'God put Adam to sleep, took a rib from his side, and created the woman.'"

"So what, do you think God went out of the business of making woman? Take a good guess. You know its people like you and me who had to decide what to put in the good book, what to leave out, and what did not need repeating over and over again. They did a good job, won't you say?"

I was flabbergasted. I had asked so many people this question and the typical answer I got was:

"Don't question the book, nobody questions the Bible."

I was dumbstruck by the simplicity and logic of his answer. "Well?"

He said getting to his feet, stretching his body to its fullest—an indication that the question and answer session was over.

"Lunchtime over, nice company. If you think of more pressing questions like this one, just stop by and ask away."

For me, I felt deep in my spirit that he had just passed the test. I got into the car and drove away with a million thoughts racing through my mind. I felt exhilarated as if I had just crossed the finishing line of a long, hard race. As I drove home, a multitude of questions particularly the one I had been carrying since my near-death experience came rushing to the forefront of my mind—the one that kept repeating itself making its way to the top of the list begging for an answer:

"Who am I?"

I was determined to ask the question on my next visit even though I felt sure that I was not yet ready to share the near-death experience that raised the question in the first place. That evening at the dinner table, my distraction was clearly visible. Keeping up with the children's usual chatter around school activities was not quite there. I waited impatiently for noontime of the following day, feeling blessed to be in the presence of this intriguing old man. To others looking on, he may seem lowly, but to me, he emitted wisdom and light. Once at the building site, however, the timing did not seem quite right to ask questions so I kept silent and listened carefully to the information the elder wanted to transmit to my husband instead. Starting up the car, there was a *feeling* that it would be wise to give full attention to what the old man had to say and the things he found it necessary to do. The timing for the asking of the next question did not seem quite right. Playing the waiting game to arrive at divine timing would soon become a part of my new communication process, a new way of life. So began the spiritual journey of a lifetime. Brother, the wisdom keeper/teacher willing to share; me, the student, open and willing to trust the wisdom of the teacher.

Deep inside of me, there was a strong sense that I had just stepped onto the threshold of an exciting and enriching spiritual journey. Was the student ready? I was not too sure about that but I was certainly determined to hang in there for the ride. In answer to my own question, there was excitement, apprehension, and certainly sufficient curiosity to kill the cat, another one of the local sayings. The next day, there was a pretty tune running through my mind and a lightness in my step. I arrived bearing a beautifully wrapped custard pie lovingly baked by the in-house chef Annabella at my home.

"Brought you a gift," I said cheerfully handing over the pie.

"So nice of you, but you didn't have to do that, so prettily wrapped too."

"Just a teaser for your sweet tooth, homemade," I said proudly.

"You bake it yourself?"

"Have to be honest, no, but my cook, Annabella got a nice sweet hand with pastry."

"That's good, you go to all that trouble just for me?"

He said shaking his head from side to side admiring the beautifully packaged pie in his hands.

"No trouble at all."

"But you see me, my wife and our whole household are strict vegetarians so I'm afraid I can't accept your gift even though it does look tempting."

He gently, but firmly placed the pie back into my hands, tipped his hat with a knowing wink in his eyes, and said lightly:

"I'm sure you understand."

"Yes I do, I should have thought of that myself, my apologies."

I took the gift from his outstretched hand, a curt smile crossed my lips. Yes, living away from home for so long, the memory of local customs had almost faded. Serious spiritual folk takes being a vegetarian to extreme levels. They do not mingle dishes or eat food prepared and/or cooked in utensils where flesh has been stored or prepared. There was no offense taken.

"So, out with the question of the day, I can sense it on the tip of your tongue."

Without stopping to think or ask how he knew there was a question to ask, it came out without any further thought.

"Brother, who am I?"

He cupped one finger around his mouth and looked at me for what seemed like a long time, then a wry smile appeared on his face.

"You want me to tell you who you are? In fact, your question is 'who am I?'"

"Yes Brother, you see I got married, took a husband, and a new last name. Then left home and family to go overseas with my new husband to live out our dreams. I was young, twenty-one years old. Saw a bit of the world, learned a lot—good things, things that changed life and living. Now we're back home with British accents, British customs, and habits. My children find it hard to fit into this Guyanese lifestyle. They are unhappy, want to go back to what they call home, London. I know I've changed, I'm confused, tell me, brother, *who am I?*"

"How long you bin asking this question in this way?" he asked

"You could say the question has been haunting me in my brain for many years now."

"So you been repeating the code only out of its natural order."

"What you mean by that?"

I fought to hold back the tears welling up inside me. Hands trembling, my feet suddenly was unsure of the ground upon which they stood. The two younger men, sitting and eating under the shade of a tree were out of earshot but paying close attention to the scene playing out before their eyes.

"I understand better than you think. Words, feelings that spring from you, but you can't see or hear the significance or the true meaning of what tortures you. More real than the hairs on your head, hmm?"

"But before we can talk about that, I got a big one for you too. Do you know or can you remember what is your birthright?"

"My birthright?" I asked perplexed.

I could not see the relevance of the question to the conversation we were having.

"Yes, your birthright. Inside of me, I feel you know the answer to that question."

I was not prepared for the comment nor my tense reaction. The question hit me in the pit of my stomach; I felt a powerful tightening across my shoulders. A feeling of dizziness caused movement backward in order to ground myself. When I opened my mouth to speak, no words came out. Somewhere deep within me, the answer was there, stifled somewhere inside. I began a mental search within my mind in an effort to find or speak the answer rising inside of me. The struggle for full expression was intense; no words were being formed. Brother on the other hand did not take his eyes off of me not even for a second. After an anxious few minutes of silence on my part, the sound began to take momentum.

"The words are stuck, can't seem to be able to come out."

"Can't or won't? Stop holding it back."

"Take a deep breath," he coached.

"Let the breath out slowly through your mouh. Breathe in slowly, out again, there."

Without taking his eyes off of me he reached out and took my trembling right hand. We took a few steps forward moving in close synchronicity in perfect timing almost as if we were dancing the tango in perfect step with each other. It felt as if our rhythms had somehow merged into the moment moving us in total togetherness. I felt myself stepping into the answer. In a very soft, almost magical voice, right there holding my right hand, he gave me his permission to speak my truth.

"Speak my child, speak your truth," he said gently.

"In your own voice."

"The one God gave to you when he sent you here."

"Speak the truth of your divine heritage."

By this time, I was sobbing; salty tears were streaming down my face and my whole body was trembling like a leaf in the wind. Finally, I mustered up enough courage almost choked on the sound streaming through my vocal chords and in an oh-so-soft whisper, much like a whimper, a single word came out as a dynamic question: *"Love?"*

"That's right, my daughter. Say it loud, say it clear, so the whole universe can hear in your own voice."

I felt energy shift within me. I cupped my two hands around my mouth and using every ounce of air I could muster up in my lungs, screamed the word *love* into the universe.

"Love!"—and the universe echoed it right back at me.

The old man's face lit up like a Christmas tree. His grip on my hand was strong. I felt love and gratitude pouring out of his heart and into mine. His face reminded me of the joy parents experience when they watch their toddler take that very first independent step.

"It is your birthright to *love* and be *loved*," he said with the brightest smile.

"Somehow, I think you won't forget it now that you've said it in your own voice."

"Now, tomorrow at noon, I'll take you to my wife; when you get there, ask her this question you been carrying for such a long time."

"Do you think she will know the answer?" I asked cautiously.

"We'll see, won't we?" he said with a twinkle in his eyes.

I arrived home in high spirits feeling confident that the answer to the question that had plagued my mind since my return from the near-death experience was about to be answered. It was a long sleepless night; I tossed and turned excitedly thinking about the next day's visit. At the break of dawn, I was up, practiced my morning meditation, and felt energized by my anticipation of the day's session. I arrived at the worksite half an hour before the scheduled departure time. I sat under a tree, observed the men at work, and marveled at the strength, level of energy, and coordination of the old man. It was Saturday and only half of a day's work was required of the crew. At exactly noon, they stopped working, gathered up their tools, boarded the truck that came to pick them up, and were off. Brother and I got into my car and drove to his "yard" as he fondly referred to as his home. I was eager to meet the other half of this lively, spiritual, wise old man. We quickly found ourselves driving away from the suburbs and into the peace of the countryside. We chit-chatted about life, about raising children; in his case, grand and great, grandchildren. He talked about what he termed as his "tribe." A collection of people numbering three generations who live on the land and off of its produce.

Eventually, we came to a stop at a large clearing upon which there was a cluster of small, basic country-style houses, probably built lovingly by worn hands, hard work, and much love. It did seem to be almost like a tribal village, the ones my grandmother told me about from her childhood. Everyone here was related to each other. They lived simple lives; the evidence of simplicity was all around me. A standpipe in the center of the cluster was their water supply. There was a small white-washed church building where I imagined the community worshipped together. I could *feel* and *sense* the love with which the children in this community was being raised. I turned off the ignition and the sweet sound of children's voices playing that age-old game of hopscotch intertwined with laughter greeted us.

The children ceased their play to turn their attention to the strange woman at the wheel of a motorcar with their elder sitting beside her. It felt as if I had driven into a picturesque scene from the early nineteen hundreds and somehow interrupted what seemed like the natural flow of a hot tropical day in the countryside. As far as the eyes could see, there were rows of crops in neat formation stretching from the back of the main house. Young men were hard at work tilling the soil. I could see smaller kitchen gardens clustered around houses. Chickens and farm animals, all a natural part of the scene before my eyes, grazed behind fences erected to limit their movement. Here and there could be seen tall majestic palm and coconut trees that framed the picture before my eyes. It was certainly a very different world from the suburbs, just a matter of twenty or so miles from where I lived. When we got out of the car, I could see that the front door to the main house was wide open. In Guyanese culture, this was a sign that I was truly welcomed to the home. An elderly woman, head beautifully wrapped in white sat comfortably in a chair just inside the front door. Brother and I were soon followed by many of the little ones as we walked up to the front door as chickens scattered to and fro to get out of our way.

"Bring a visitor to see you," Brother called out loudly.

"Dis is my new student Norma. She got questions, boy does she have questions, she got a special one just fuh you."

He turned to me and nodded in the direction of his wife.

"Dis is sister, everyone around here call us brother and sister, of the church, of course."

I stepped forward to shake her outstretched hand. It was as warm as her welcoming smile. The smell of lavender, my favorite scent, tickled my nose bringing a hint of joy and remembrance of my dear grandmother to the moment. There was a familiarity about the moment that made my heart quicken and a feeling that this meeting was predestined. I could not shake the strange feeling that I had walked in step with this person somewhere, sometime in the past. I tried hard to curb the excitement brought on by the memory and wondered if she could *feel* a strong energy too.

Sister, as everyone fondly called her, was shorter than I imagined her to be. The next thing that I noticed about her was her eyes— bright and shining like a pair of twinkling stars in the night sky. The grey in her hair was almost in contrast to her smooth, wrinkle-free skin, and perfect natural brown complexion. She was alive with energy. My attention was also drawn to her feet; these were small and dainty and said something positive to me about her personality.

Her smile matched the radiance of the aura of light I could discern around her physical body. At the crown chakra, a circle of golden light could be discerned.

"Pleased to meet you," she said laughing.

"I *see* you," she added, her finger pointing toward my heart chakra.

I understood what she meant. It was an old African statement indicating that one can read the other person's spirit. I proceeded with my own response to her greeting with a bright smile.

"I *see* you too. It's a pleasure and a blessing to be in your presence."

That was me acknowledging to her that I could clearly see her spirituality too. Brother perched himself comfortably on the steps and a large brown dog enthusiastically appeared by his side, licking his face in a warm greeting. He encouraged the children to return to their play and they did, not without casting enquiring glances back at the doorway where the dog and the three adults sat in conversation. Turning to his wife, Brother said:

"She's got one of them woman-to-woman questions, so I bring her to you."

"What is it, my daughter? Ask."

Her bright eyes seemed to penetrate every aspect of my being. I was sure that in that intense gaze, she probably could have told me my past, my present, as well as my future. I was comforted by the gentle look in her eyes but something told me to refrain from asking questions about what she saw in me. I smiled politely and kept my thoughts to myself.

"Tell sister today's burning question," Brother prompted.

I took a deep breath, composed myself, not wanting to seem too eager or emotional, and said:

"It's very simple really . . . I want to know *who I am*."

"Hmm, that's a big one."

She fell silent for a few minutes. It seemed to me that she effortlessly disengaged her spirit from her physical body to gaze off into the distance. A respectful few minutes of silence followed. There was a void at the moment as I waited breathlessly for her answer. When she cleared her throat, I knew that I again had her full attention after a brief disassociation. She turned to me and with a *knowingness* in her eyes said:

"Go home, think about your question, and next Sabbath day I will come to your home. Give the servants the day off, I want to visit you and your family. We'll put our heads together to get to the bottom of your little mystery."

"Thank you so very much," I said bowing graciously.

I knew she meant that her visit would be on the next Saturday. Most spiritual people in Guyana honor Saturday as the "Holy Sabbath" day. I said my appropriate goodbyes to the adults, patted the dog, acknowledged the children on my way back to the car, and made my way home. I was really overjoyed at the simplicity and peacefulness of the meeting. In my traditional culture, the elderly do not pay visits to the young. It was the other way around—the young visits the old. I felt really honored that she would grace my home with the brilliance of her light and her spiritual presence; more importantly that she would make the visit on her Sabbath day.

Sister arrived at our home early on that Saturday morning accompanied by seven female elders. They entered the home with a joyful singing of songs of praises and in-between singing, they gave thanks to God that a son and daughter of the soil had returned back into the fold of the local community. After suitable introductions that were made, Sister said to my husband:

"Please show us around your beautiful home."

After her requested tour of the home was completed, we all returned to the living room. Here, she complimented my husband on the quality of the home he had provided for his family. To me, her compliments were for the standard cleanliness and the quality of the décor of the home. Then, she snapped her fingers, and the elders who had accompanied her sprang into action. They began to carefully unhang the artwork from the walls in the living room. My treasured crystal collection displayed on glass shelving under controlled lighting was put away with great care. The shelves quickly dismantled and laid out on the floor while the crystals were wrapped in newspaper and put in boxes which they brought with them. Family pictures and artifacts were set on the sofas; every piece of furniture was pulled to the center of the room. She requested bed linens which were used as covers. Our living room now looked as if we were ready for movers. I was, needless to say, speechless, unsure of what was really going on. I swallowed hard, forcing myself to remain calm under the circumstances so as to sound as polite as possible.

"Can we help, be of assistance in what you are doing?"

"Oh no," was her lighthearted response.

"Your task right now is to watch, listen, and learn."

My husband and I looked at each other in total disbelief. Sister's tone was however very comforting as she returned to directing the task at hand. With gospel choruses on their lips, lighthearted banter, and laughter, the elders proceeded to do the same for every room in the house. They moved the furniture to the center of each room, placing a covering of sheets over the assembled items. When they got to the study where the walls were lined with accolades, degrees, and plaques that commemorated our success in London—all of these were placed on the floor face upward and left uncovered. In a couple of hours, the house looked ready for a moving crew. I was too afraid to ask what the next steps in this arduous process might be.

As soon as the dismantling was complete, she took my hand in hers, walked me back to the living room where this elaborate exercise had started, and in that oh-so-melodious voice of hers invitingly said:

"Come, my daughter, let's walk through your house."

I instantly made a mental note that what she initially called *home* had now become just a house.

"You ask the question, my child, who am I?"

Her tone was melancholy but also very gentle as she repeated the statement.

"You ask the question, 'who am I?' I can *feel* the depth of your search for the answer."

Suddenly, I was sobbing uncontrollably. It was as if a well of emotions had somehow been allowed to move to the surface of my mind.

"Yes," I whispered between sobs.

"Tell me please, who am I?"

"I can't answer that question for you. That's yours and yours only to answer."

"Tell me Sister who am I?" I pleaded.

"I can only help you the best way I know how," was her gentle response.

"By reminding you of who you are not. Now, let's take another walk through your house."

We re-entered the living room and she prefaced her entry into every room with these words:

"Lest you forget my child, let me walk you through an important reminder."

We moved in rhythm, her outstretched hand gesturing toward the artifacts stacked in the center of the living room.

"This is a reminder of who you are not. Things in and of themselves are not good or bad. It is when we see ourselves, measure ourselves through the eyes of the things we have collected in our life. That's the point when material things become a problem and lead us into confusion."

I looked at her in surprise, she was, it seemed, about to teach me a valuable lesson using my own treasured possessions as the props.

"What value have you given to these things in your life? What I mean is the way you treasure these material things has become your storehouse of treasure, your mark of distinction and could well be in the way of you discerning who you really are."

I found myself not only listening keenly but also soaking up the words into my mind as well as in my spirit. It was clearly another spiritually defining moment in my life. Our entry into each room was prefaced with the same words. When we got to the study, she deliberately paused, looked me deep in the eyes, and gestured to the pile of certificates, degrees and accolades lying on the floor of the study, then she said:

"And this," pointing to the stuff on the floor, "is definitely not who you are at this moment. Perhaps . . . maybe later on in life, you may live up to the lessons taught by these worldly pieces of paper, but for now, it's what the world says you are capable of. Strive, my child, to make these words come alive in your life, make them real. But remember, putting Almighty God first, dig deep inside yourself to find the light and integrity that lives within you. Then remind yourself every step of the way that you came into this life the way we all have come with a divine purpose. Back that up with the pureness of your intentions. When you have done that, my daughter, only then can you truly claim these credits as your own."

"How, Sister, tell me how to do this, you're showing me now, but teach me, please."

I felt her words penetrating deeply into my very soul. When we returned to the living room, she complimented us as a married couple for being gracious hosts and good sports. Next, she reminded me to be careful of creating and giving allegiance to altars full of physical objects such as the one I had of shimmering crystal with artificial light highlighting the beauty of the crystals. I had not up untilmoment seen the dsplay as an altarbut I acknowledged in the moment that the reverence I had afforded the display turned it into a space of reverence and adoration. Sister continued.

"Remember, from this day onwards, that reverence and allegiance belongs to the Creator of the Universe."

"Yes, Sister," was my humble response.

"Now I want you to look me in the eye when you repeat these simple words. They mean a lot more than they sound. 'I am that I am.'" She made me repeat those words seven times.

With those words said, she bowed graciously to us and to the waiting female elders in the living room and bade us goodbye. This story is now a part of our family history. It is shared by me or often through the eyes of my two eldest children at family gatherings and now I have shared it with you, my readers. Is there a message hidden in this exercise, among the words spoken that could possibly speak to your own search?

This exercise shaped the way in which I journeyed through my own 'middle passage' my desert experience—those most challenging times in and of my life. The work of self-discovery started that day; it spanned two amazing decades of my life. The journey through the desert brought challenges too many to mention here, divinely inspired moments, teachers, messengers, healers, and a number of earth-angels into my life.

Once I was clear about who I was not on this journey called life, Brother took me on a journey of self-discovery which took off like a house on fire. He took the time to trace my life from a spiritual perspective; my ancestral line, moved me through the lineage, and led me to sift through the relationships that framed my life and my perspective. We did serious work on respecting the body as the temple of the living God, the mind as a reservoir of knowledge and information and the eternal soul that belongs to Almighty God.

"Just because you got knowledge up here," pointing to my head, "doesn't mean you know how to live it out in this life here and now."

In a class that I attended that he taught, he began the session with these piercing words:

"Know ye not that the body is the temple of the living God?"

The statement grabbed my attention as he continued with the words:

"And God gave to man dominion over all living things . . . since then man has lost his way by eating up the flesh from off of the earth."

It was not so much what he said but the authority in his voice when he said it that caught and held my attention. That was on a Friday evening. By Monday, I was a non-flesh eating vegetarian and have continued to this day well over forty or so years later.

By the time the clearing of the land and construction of our new home was complete, my relationship with this couple had become unique. They became teachers/coaches to me in helping me to 'walk the spiritual talk.' First, there was usually an instruction that provided information; next, there were the physical exercises that framed the journey to spiritual freedom. The next step on the agenda proved to be mastering the spiritual clearing, cleansing, and grounding processes to render my mind and my body fitting vessels for the use of the Holy Spirit. I continually marveled at the purity of their energy and the calmness of their spirits. Brother, I discovered, to my amazement, was in fact ninety-years-old and his wife eighty-three. They led very active, energetic lives, were elders of their tribe, spiritual teachers to me and many others in their community, and deemed as wisdom keepers on the planet. This amazing teacher/student relationship continued for five years of my life. During all of the time I spent studying with them, the family continued our membership and worship at the local Episcopal Church.

In the meantime, Brother took two years to walk me through the spiritual understanding of the Old Testament of the Bible. His wife took three years to open me up to the mysteries to be found in the New Testament. She was a natural, gifted teacher who allowed the spirit to be her guide. She was and still is in my memory one of the most compassionate people I ever had the privilege to know. Her work with children from all walks of life still stands out in my memory. In a third world country where there are three major religions, Hinduism, Islam, and Christianity, and poverty where medical care is not readily available in rural areas, she saved the lives of many children. It mattered not to her from which religion they came. I watched her take very sick, undernourished children into her home. She anointed them, nurtured, prayed over them, and breathed the breath of Almighty God into their lungs when necessary. When they gained strength and vitality, she returned healthy children back into the arms of grateful mothers. It was such an example of unconditional love and faith in action. In response to my questions about the source of the healings, I witnessed she would say:

"We live with the Holy Spirit and the light of Christ in our hearts and in our homes. Anyone or anything that dwells here in this home even for a short time will be touched by the presence of God and the light of Christ. Remember the scripture—'Ask and it shall be given unto you.' choose to live a life of compassion, and of service, and you will see miracles begin to happen before your eyes. These babies are living examples of Christ's words."

It was as if I was a witness to a transformation process that embodied the terms 'rags to riches.' Their mothers often brought their babies wrapped in rags; they would stay awhile for ten days, sometimes as long as a month. Sister kept them close to her breast, strapped them onto her back or her chest as she performed her daily chores. They slept with her, she anointed them in prayer and sang songs of praises to them. The church community made them clothing and comforted their mothers while Brother made healing herbal balms that brought healing and comfort to their wounds. Eventually, I'd watch them returned to their mothers with the richness and blessings of good health and a chance to live out a full life. In a country where, at the time, the death rate for babies born in poor, rural communities from dysentery and often malnutrition was high, this labor of love was indeed a blessing from above. Services were rendered freely without any cost to the families.

Brother's mission, on the other hand, seemed to me was to teach, change, and empower lives. He was a preacher, a farmer, a gravedigger, a healer, and a life coach to many. In his own life, he practiced and taught the art of serious discipline that became living examples to those around him and thereby transformed lives.

"Give me one generation," Brother would say, "and I'll show you God's healing hand at work with better than good results handed down to the third and fourth generation."

"If we walk the talk, we earn the right to break the yoke of poverty and ignorance with the word and the discipline of sacredness."

Brother and Sister were uneducated by the world's standards. By those same standards, they were looked upon as impoverished. Yet, from my observation, they lacked nothing and did not need the trimmings of the world to bring about their state of joy and happiness. Peace, joy, and happiness just ousted out of their souls, into their lives, and the lives of those around them.

It was amazing to me to observe the way in which Brother responded to deep spiritual questions. It was always with a simple exercise that was often demonstrated as drawings in the sand. So it was when he introduced me to the spiritual exercise of fasting. He drew in the sand a simple drawing of the internal journey of food moving through the body. He then reminded me that even though it seemed like an automatic system, it took an amazing amount of energy to accomplish the task of digestion.

"Do a twenty-four-hour fast and after the time it takes the food to digest, you are left with energy that is used to clear, cleanse, repair, and relax the body. Got that?"

"Yes, I think I do."

I said seriously keenly studying the simple drawing before me in the sand.

"When you relax, there is energy flowing through the system. You can now still yourself enough to listen to the inner world."

"But what about feeling the pangs of hunger?" I asked

"That is natural when you first begin to fast. With practice, the mind overrides matter and with your good intentions for the fast, hunger will soon fade away."

The look on my face must have shown my disagreement with his theory.

"It depends . . . what is your intention, your purpose for fasting? For you, right now you want to sincerely, I hope, enter into the inner chambers to listen and be in tune with your spirit, learn first hand about your purpose, yes?"

"Yes, something like that."

Is that search, it is the burning need to uncover your purpose, that will hold you to sticking to the fast. Yes?" He looked at me directly in the eyes.

His intense scrutiny seemed to me to determine the strength of my intention. He must have been satisfied with what he saw so he continued.

"So we begin with twenty-four hours, sun up to sundown, and work our way up to three days."

"Yes sir," was my response.

This conversation became the foundation for my journey of fasting to attain inner focus, purpose, and to strengthen my resolve and intention. Before long, I was doing a three-day fast quite easily. Fasting for me tended to bring questions and unexplained concepts to the forefront of my mind. So one day, Brother and I had an interesting conversation.

"Brother, I said if God loves us so much, how is it that there are all these disasters around the world, why is it that God is not taking better care of humanity?"

"So, you think God is shirking his responsibilities, hmm?"

"Well, look at the world?" I responded hesitantly.

"Go back to our lesson on thoughts how they turn into words; words spoken with intention good or bad bring about reality. Remember we talked about the chair you were sitting, on being a thought that turned into words that created and directed energy that brought about the physical reality of creating a chair."

"Yes sir," was my rapid-fire response.

"So let's go to the source of this question. Action speaks louder than words."

"What do you mean?" I asked puzzled.

"So give me a forty-day fast, its the best way I know of to get answers directly from the Source."

"Forty days?" My face showed the shock and disbelief I felt.

"No one can survive without eating real food for that long," was my response.

"I want to remind you that you live among Muslims who carry a forty-day fast during Ramadan every year."

This statement shut me up for indeed, all my school life, I attended classes with Muslim children who fasted for forty days and came to school and functioned well throughout the fast.

"Get yourself up before sunrise, eat a slice of bread made without yeast, a cup of herbal tea, and fruit. Offer up prayers, spend time in meditation and in silence, then go about your usual chores sipping water throughout the day," he instructed.

"At sunset, break the fast with a cup of broth made of vegetables and bread. Again prayers, meditation, silence, and listen, listen, listen."

My perplexity must have shown on my face, so he continued:

"You really hungry for answers, I can *feel* it. You got to tame that monster inside with discipline, master the fine art of listening, softly, quietly to the universe, to the spirit within. Now if it means that you have to change the way you run your life, that's your job to do, not mine I'm only the teacher, you're the seeker of truth."

"Yes sir."

The statement was made with just a hint of sarcasm, but I knew in my heart that I would try it.

Ten days before the end of the fast, he added a new caveat:

"For the last seven days of the fast, pray three times each day, do not swallow your saliva, spit it out. Allow the body to experience deliverance, and the spirit to feast on prayer."

At the end of the forty-day fast, too weak to stand for very long, I was driven over to my teacher's yard by a friend. There he was deep in conversation with a young man; he turned and with raised eyebrows, he looked at me. Asked to be excused from his conversation with his visitor and in a somber voice, he said:

"Excuse me," he said to the gentleman with whom he was conversing and turned to me with faked surprise in his voice.

"So you survived. Who kept you alive while you starved your body of food and water?"

"Were you starved of that vital thing called oxygen? Who kept body, mind, soul, and spirit together? Experience really does teach wisdom. Does it not?"

He said with the sternness leaving his face; he smiled. I was too weak and embarrassed to argue or offer up words or an opinion.

"Oh! Just so you know I kept the fast right alongside you."

He placed his hands lovingly around my shoulder and hugged me.

"Thank you," I whispered.

"We are never going to examine this question of yours about whether God takes care of his own again, right?"

"No Sir, I got it," I answered nodding my head, "got the answer, understand it."

Now, let me take you to Sister so we both can have a hearty meal to break our fast.

This fasting from food was accompanied by four hours of daily silence. It forced me to wake up at four-thirty each morning to hold an hour of silence before the family woke up. At lunchtime, I would hold the entire hour in silence. Last thing before bedtime, I would carry the last two hours of silence. Brother required me to give up the fast from food but keep the fast from words, emgaging fours hours of silence a day for three years of my life. His guidance allowed me to take meditation to another level and helped me to identify and breakdown walls of resistance born of stubbornness and my surrender to worldly ways. I emerged with a brand new perspective.

Guiding me inward through meditation and contemplation without any material or ulterior motive took me to the point of conscious alignment with the universe. Sitting in nature, I could *feel* the love flowing in and through the universe. These exercises brought purity and clarity into my life. One day, I asked my teacher why it was that I could not remember my past lives in the order in which I had lived them. We were sitting in nature in his cabbage patch when I asked the question. He called his granddaughter and requested her to bring him the following items—a pair of rubber gloves, a clean glass, a pair of scissors, and the garden hose. At the sight of the assembled items, I was more than a little baffled.

"Now," he said.

"Hook up the hose. Put the nozzle of the hose inside the glove. Turn on the water and draw me a glass of water."

The water came tumbling out of the top of the glove making it difficult to fill the glass.

"Now turn off the water, take the scissors, and cut a hole at the bottom of each finger of the glove. Put the hose back into the glove and turn on the water and then fetch me a glass of water."

The water poured out of the created holes allowing me to effortlessly fill the glass with water. Holding the filled glass of water up to the sunlight, he said.

"Crystal clear glass of water, don't you agree?"

"Yes," was my immediate response

"Now, turn the hose off, remove the nozzle from the glove."

"Pick up five pebbles, put one in each finger of the glove. Grab a handful of dirt and put in a little bit into each finger of the glove."

I took great care in following the instruction that I was given to the letter.

"Now turn back on the hose, place the nozzle back into the glove. Now draw me a glass of water from the bottom of one of the fingers of the glove."

The water entered into the glove, most of it overflowed from the top of the glove making a mess; next, a slow trickle of dirty water oozed out of the bottom of the glove. It took quite a while before there was a full glass of water. I handed it to him with something of a scowl on my face. He held it up towards the light.

"How do you say this nicely?" he asked.

"Polluted, dirty water," I responded.

"Can't do nothing with it. Can't wash me hands or me face, much less drink it."

He instructed me to turn off the hose and invited me to:

"Turn on your brain, let's see what you thinking."

"If you want clean water to drink, would it make sense to take it from the standpipe?"

"That's true but right now, you are only on the surface with your thinking. Let's see."

"You want to know why you can't remember your past lives, correct?"

"Yes, I do want to know," was the answer that popped out of my mouth.

"So, I got to interpret this fuh you. The glove we start off with has no holes, no pebbles, no dirt, but also no openings right?"

"That's right," I said in return more than a little baffled.

"That was like the unborn baby in the womb. With all the information you looking for tightly wrapped up inside the baby."

I was still baffled, seeking an internal image to help my understanding.

"But you see, the baby had a strong purpose, a big goal if you want to call it that."

"And that was?"

"Being born, struggling to get into your world," was his response.

"Now, glove with opening, a way to understand the birth canal. There is an opening; it can now deliver sparkling, clear water. Birth canal ready to deliver the newborn into the world. Information flowing in and through the birth canal."

I did not quite understand the theory and he could sense that I was struggling.

"Glove with a clear passage that gives the opportunity of free-flow or passage into this life?"

I offered the information haltingly, not sure that I had quite got it right.

"Right, but now there is a problem."

Brother continued his eyes fixed on my puzzled face.

"But now there's a problem."

"What is the problem?"

"The glove, or for that matter, the sack with the information, is tangled up with all of this dirt that has been dumped in the way. No flow, right?"

"No flow, that's right."

It was as if a light bulb went on in my head and brought illumination.

"So then, the dirt we dumped on top of the pure information is what's in the way. It's blocking the flow."

"You way smarter than you think, my child."

"So, where, how did dirt get into a newborn baby that fast?"

"Babies process everything they hear while inside of their mother's womb. Added to that from the second of birth, they also begin to suck up information from everyone and everything all around them. They look for information from the world they just got into. Belief systems, joy, pain, everything they can find to help them to survive here on earth. What starts off as pure soon become . . . what's that fancy word you use?"

"Toxic?"

"Ah, that's the word I was looking for. I say tainted."

"So how do we get the dirt out of the way?" I asked seriously.

"Now you ask the right question. That's the *work*—the spiritual work that got to be done, to clear the way for enlightenment."

I nodded becoming aware of the emerging truth behind what Brother was trying to explain. He continued to enlighten me.

"First, you got to wake up, and I got to give it to you, that you are awake. The next step are the teachings and practice to take you inside yourself. Next comes clearing and cleansing. It's the way for all spiritual seekers of truth. It's about making way so the *truth* can shine through. We, God's people, we all got work to do."

"How? Where do we begin? How do we know what to purge and what to keep?"

"You ahead of me, slow down, you moving too fast," he said.

"You know that scripture? The one that goes like this . . . you must be born again . . . find it for me in this Bible here."

I was now really puzzled and asked questions with a genuine interest in the answers.

"Before you confuse yourself with your own questions, know that your very next step, my child, is baptism. Wash the past away, rise from the water renewed. A real baptism."

"You mean there's more than one type of baptism?"

"Yes, there is. True baptism goes with the ebb and flow of the tide and the salt of the sea to wash away stubbornness, transgressions, and wild imaginings stored within. Some call it sin. We have to make way for the truth and nothing but the truth. Some say it is just for clearing sin and stop right there. It's true, sin is sin, but its only a part of the preparation to receive the new spiritual seed. Think of the burdens/habits you may be carrying from your childhood memories or for that matter, the many lives you have lived."

I was surprised to hear this Christian preacher talk so freely about past lives, but then again, I reminded myself that he was schooled by the African elders on the spiritual threads to be found in the Holy Bible.

"Sea salt," he continued, "is one of the most powerful cleansers on earth. And, the *spirit of God* fills and fulfills."

"What does that mean?" I asked.

"Let's see, walk your talk, live long enough, and you'll come to *know* the answer."

Brother discerned that it was not his assigned task to baptize me so he and his wife took me on a long trip deep into the countryside. We took a two-hour taxi ride that put us off at the beginning of a steep, rough country road from where we had to walk another mile or so. We arrived at our destination unannounced, tired, and a little breathless at Elder John's house. We were greeted by his wife who offered us refreshments as we waited patiently for Elder John's arrival home. Soon, we heard a rich, deep baritone voice greeting the next-door neighbor. A dog barking excitedly was running up and down the stairs as if to announce our presence. When Elder John entered the doorway, he looked directly at me as if the other members of the party were non-existent. He greeted me with these words:

"Where have you been?" His eyes were searching my face for an answer.

"I've been waiting for you for a long time. I thought you'd never show up," he said.

Before I could answer, Brother provided the answer with a chuckle:

"England! She went and sailed the seas and come back to meet you."

"No wonder it took you so long, my daughter. What business did you have there?"

"Married and went there to get an education."

He threw his head back and laughed heartily.

"And now you here to be born again?"

He then turned and greeted Brother and his wife and we prepared for the trip to the ocean.

Before long, there was a party of seven of us headed toward the Atlantic Ocean. We marched on humming hymns along the way. People in the little country houses by the wayside came out to stand on the side of the road; they waved and blessed us on our way. They were all fully aware that we were heading to the sea to conduct a baptism. When the procession got to the ocean, the tide was high. Just before we entered the water, the baptizing elder gave me these instructions:

"You got teachings and instructions from your elder, yes?"

"Yes, Sir, I did," was my response.

"Based on what you have come to know, what you have found from going within, I call on you to empty your head and mind of your thoughts and speak your soul's clear intention for your baptism."

Then, he took me down three times, first in the name of the Father (surface), and of the Son (surface), and of the Holy Spirit. When I surfaced for the last time, I heard myself affirm in that voice I had come to know as my *own voice* stating my innermost convictions above the roar of the ocean.

"A charge to keep have I
A God to glorify—A never-dying soul to save
And fit it for the sky."

We waded out of the water, he with the hundred and twenty-first Psalm on his lips with my first name inserted to personalize the moment. He then spoke those precious words my grandmother had sung when I surrendered my life and I knew that her spirit was there present with us.

"The cross before you,
The world behind you—no turning back, no turning back."

A wave of utter and blissful peace spread over my entire being. Then, standing facing me, his face seeming quite perplexed, the baptizing elder made a statement that shocked us all:

"You are a priest in the Order of Melchizedek."

The statement gushed out of him; his surprise was obvious at the depth of the words that came out of his mouth. The Order of Melchizedek is an order of priests identified in the Old Testament of the Bible.

"What, where did that come from?" was my puzzled question.

"What does it mean?"

"Hush, my daughter, enough of the questions," the elder said in a soothing voice.

"Everything, every prophecy will be revealed in God's time."

References in the Old Testament of the Bible to this order of the priesthood of Melchizedek always intrigued me. It seemed so far removed from my present-day life that I should be associated in any way with such an ancient order.

"You will be shown in a dream who it is that will ordain you. It is not my *rite* nor have I been chosen for the task. My job right here and now is like that of John the Baptist to prepare the way."

I was kept awake all that night in the little church close to the ocean. The elders of the community came out to keep the *watch* with us. Sweet old-time hymns and choruses rang out in-between biblical instructions; female voices anchored by the deep bass voices of the male elders rang out until sunrise. Specially selected scripture and ancient readings were also read to me. The science behind the ancient saying with which I was always fascinated, 'As above: So below' was painstakingly explained to me.

"As your life has been planned in the spirit world before you came here; so it would be lived out from this day forward."

This saying he explained is at the root of New Testament teachings on "surrender." It means total surrender to the universal plan that leads to the fulfillment of purpose "here on earth as it is decreed in heaven."

I was forcefully reminded at that moment of my mother's response to Aunt Sarah's prophesy:

"Time will tell."

The memory allowed me to open up and accept what was being foretold to me. I felt so much love in that little church that night. I found myself moved to tears at several points during the anointing and prayers. The very next night, a powerful image came to me in my meditation session. It was the face of a white male. I knew instinctively that he was the one who was designated to conduct my ordination. Both Brother and Sister were absolutely delighted by the prophecy as well as the "sighting" as they called it of the one who was destined to ordain me. They in turn organized and conducted in their little church magical praise and thanksgiving celebration service of light *and love* that in their own words they termed as the turning on of the "light codes" within. This was in honor and celebration of the journey before me.

"My child," Brother said.

"You've been blessed by a visit from the 'angel of mercy' and the time has come to step out into the world and teach. We give you all we could. You're now ready to step out into the world, to teach, to set the captives free, and to open up the eyes of those who are ready for the change that is to come."

"I'm not so sure about being ready," I murmured.

"Sounds like you are kicking me out into the world are you?" I asked suddenly feeling very sorry for myself.

"Yes, we are," they said in unison with a distinct level of confidence.

"Ships look good sitting in the harbor, but ships are meant to sail the seas."

I sat in prayer, fasting and meditating for seven days contemplating my faith. While I was doing that, Brother and Sister were celebrating my graduation from what they called a "period of instruction" to what they perceived as the beginning of my "journey to mastery." I have to admit that it was the one time I did not quite agree with their sentiments.

Soon after this very spiritual experience, I woke up one morning filled with a *knowing* that indeed the next phase of my life's journey was upon me. A very urgent need sprang up inside of me to look at the possibility of moving the family out of Guyana. This came as a surprise to those around me including my husband. My argument against migration particularly to America had always been that children should at all cost be protected from the intensity of racism. As we discussed the possibility of the move, two very strong intentions surfaced. The first of which was to discharge our parental responsibility of providing higher education for our four children. The second was to follow and fulfill my life's purpose, even though at that time, I did not quite know as yet what that purpose was. Throughout the planning and exploratory stages, my husband was extremely belligerent. However, despite his fear of becoming just another *black man* in America, with fervent prayer, we pursued and was granted visas for both England and America. His mother, a longstanding American citizen, sponsored the family.

Upon acquiring legal immigration visas for both countries, I remember placing the two passports side by side and asking God for direction. Later that night during meditation, it was placed upon my heart that the United States of America was the preferred destination. I awoke to share this information with my husband. He was still rigidly opposed to the idea of leaving the roots we had established in Guyana. We decided to take a three-month vacation and traveled to America to visit his mother and most of his siblings who lived there. It was, however, evident to me that the purpose of the vacation was to learn about American culture, to have in-depth discussion with family members in the USA, and to investigate the potential for acquiring jobs here and educating our children. However, my husband again stressed that to him, the trip was just a vacation and that he had no intention of immigrating. By choice, he had managed to remain distant from the spiritual side of my life which he deemed rather questionable. His priority was, he declared, that while on vacation in America, I should seek out a psychological evaluation. I had therefore refrained from sharing any of my spiritual revelations with my husband.

During this reflective time of my life, the subject of seminary popped up often in my meditation. My husband objected to and remained unwilling to support any effort that would take me to seminary. His objections were firmly based on St. Paul's famous words "let your women keep silence in the church." There was no reasoning in the world that seemed able to shift him from his belief in the matter. I have to admit that I too was deeply influenced by those words that caused me to question/doubt my suitability for the prophecy that clearly hung over my head. So, we began our vacation with the understanding that immigration and/or staying in America was not on the table. Suffice it to say that fate had another plan and three months later, we were frantically packing for the shift from Guyana to America. It took vigilant prayer, a strong faith, and the weight of prophecy to eventually get us to America.

CHAPTER EIGHT

Every student on a spiritual quest long for the reading and a blessing from the spiritual teacher. Sister and Brother's last words of blessings to me the day before we left Guyana came out as part-prophecy, part-spiritual reading. In a strange way, it brought sadness as well as comfort to my spirit. First, Sister placed the palm of her hand on the crown of my head. Next, she lit a candle and held it gracefully between us in her right hand as we stood facing each other.

"It is better to light a candle than to stumble around in the dark," she said.

"This candle is lit first of all to lighten your heart and your burden; secondly, as a lamp unto your feet. Bless you, my daughter."

A feeling of complete peace spread throughout my entire being. I stood there patiently waiting for her next words, for her proclamation, and I was oblivious of time or consequence. Her eyes took me in as if she was seeing me for the very first time. The steady flow of the words fell upon me with the smooth ease of a babbling brook. She closed her eyes.

"Hmm."

She sighed deeply as if what she was sensing and seeing behind her closed eyelids was a burden to bear.

"America is waiting, holding your biggest and deepest challenges, yet the prophesy of ordination will be fulfilled there. My daughter, ask God Almighty to help you to keep these hands of yours clean so that like King David, you can ask God to do unto you according to the cleanliness of your hands."

These words came to me as if from a far-off place from where it seemed she was actively receiving the message she willingly voiced. Shaking her head sadly from side to side to demonstrate her disillusionment at what she was perceiving, she continued:

"The road ahead is going to be rough. You will face trials, tribulations, deceit, and rejections as soon as you get to America. Don't be too quick to cast blame, for your period of testing is upon you; can you keep your eyes on higher ground when everything around you is falling apart? In your journey with us, we talked a lot about faith. Those who guide and guard you in the spiritual realms will now take the opportunity to observe and let you know the faith with which you now walk. How strong, how deep is your faith? The next milestone demands that you be grounded. Remember, my child, the amazing power of prayer; talk to God, better still listen for his direction. Where he leads, follow. In your trials, ask that your feet be set firmly on the path that leads to righteousness. There you will leave loneliness behind to step into your purpose. Before you always, there will be right and wrong. To move forward requires you to choose. Do the right thing, even if it costs you money, earthly treasures, and/ or sacrifice of time, and the God you serve will make a way for you. Do it all for the glory of Almighty God. If you work at it diligently in your elder years, with chaos all around you, you will *know* peace and take your place among the wisdom keepers on this earth until he calls you home."

It was the only time in our five years of interaction that Sister ever did what is called a "reading" for me. I watched her "read" for others, guide others to their destiny, but she would say to me that I had the ability to talk/listen to God so there was no need for her to "read" my life's journey. In the midst of her "reading," my heart became heavy and tears of sadness began streaming down my face. Her expression also spoke to me of sadness, but in a strange way, the words she spoke brought comfort as well. She continued her reading on a different and lighthearted note.

"When you get to this place they call America—oh so much paper—how many trees did they have to chop down to make so much paper? They got big, big houses too with so many people going in and out of only one front door. How do they live like that? Everybody there is in a big hurry, even the cars and trains full of people hurrying."

At the time of her reading, Guyana had no television and she had never been to a movie theatre, so she was in fact seeing life in America through spiritual eyes and relating what she saw so clearly.

"You going back to school again, cha, cha," she said in astonishment.

"Reallly?" I responded a little confused.

"This trip is about education for the children," I responded.

"Hmm, I see you going back to get another piece of paper with a gold star on it."

She was baffled and so was I. Not being an educated woman, she did not know she was referring to a doctoral degree. She continued her reading.

"When you done with all that school, take yourself to the ocean, my child; go when the tide is going out. Squat, my daughter, remember how you pushed those babies out into the world. Breathe and push, my daughter," she said with great emphasis.

"What am I pushing out, Sister?"

I asked breathlessly for I felt as if I was in a strange way already bearing down to save my life.

"All the knowledge they gonna put into that head of yours, the parts you don't need to do Almighty God's bidding. Spiritual work is handed down from above and is directed by the angels. The Creator will preserve all that you need, all that is necessary to your work on the planet, then he will reorder your steps according to his will."

There was a visible shift in her emotions as she narrated this. Shaking her head from side to side as if in disbelief, she opened her eyes in wide wonderment—that beautiful smile of hers that warmed my heart whenever I saw it burst forth.

"It's God's will that you experience marriage twice. This first one is really only just a legal contract. The second, the real marriage, will be the love and support of your life and you will be made ready to *know* what true love really is."

At the time, it was true that there were problems in the marriage. I had, however, at that point in my marriage never entertained the thought of divorce so I assumed that I would be widowed.

And from Brother, simple but sacred words, for I knew in my spirit that he, being at the age of over ninety, it would be the last time I would hear the sound of his rich baritone voice.

"We'll be here, and there," he said pointing to the sky, "watching and praying with you always. You will do more there in America than you could ever do here in your own land. Remember, my child, a prophet is never a prophet in his or her own land."

I did not quite understand that statement when it was voiced; I do now.

"It's never goodbye," he continued, "remember, we all connected by the mighty chords of Almighty God's love."

We hugged—Brother, Sister, and the family. Brother said the final prayer for blessings and traveling mercies. When we parted, I was careful not to look back. I could not; it was far too emotional. Some magical things only happen once in a lifetime so I gently closed the door with a grateful heart. I knew that I had been well equipped to journey the rest of the way on what today I have come to consider as the proverbial "road less traveled."

I begged my teachers to accompany the family to the airport at our expense but they both declined. I understood that they were letting go to let God guide the journey before me. One of the fundamentals of his teaching that he repeated to me over and over again was:

"Let go; let God."

When in his opinion I had asked too many basic questions, his response would be:

"Are you questioning the wisdom of the God who created and continue to rule the heavens and the earth? Tell me, you think he needs me and you to tell him how to clean up the grains of sand that is us humans, that is a part of his creation?"

Brother and Sister never left that little town in which they were born where they grew up and gave their talent, bringing healing to all those whom they were called to serve. It had been a tremendous blessing for me to witness, feel, and taste the depth of their spiritual presence, their unwavering faith, and their joy on the planet. It was, for me, the witness of a labor of love that demonstrated the meaning of the biblical statement—"Love your neighbor as yourself."

During the family's last twenty-four hours in Guyana, I found myself appreciating the intensity and learning curve of "walking the spiritual talk." That was Brother's term for the rigid discipline and surrender to Almighty God that he believed with all of his heart was a necessary part of redemption.

"Knowing the way," he would say, "is one thing. Stumbling over the pitfalls along the way is how it is that we move from understanding to overstanding the way. It's the place where wisdom begins."

I was overcome with gratitude for all the information transferred into me by these two wisdom keepers. They refused to allow me to repay them with the world's money so I turned my eyes heavenward and asked God's richest blessings upon them and the tribe of which they were the elders. To this day, whenever the memory crosses my mind, I continue to ask for the richest and most abundant blessings to fall upon them wherever they may be in the universe.

With our entire household reduced to six suitcases and our two loving and devoted dogs assigned to new homes, we were as ready as we could for the next phase of life.

CHAPTER NINE

Goodbyes for me once again proved difficult. Leaving family, my trusted and loyal household staff, and the community behind tore at my very soul. I had tried as best as I could to place the staff in suitable households. So it was that on a bright, tropical morning, the sun shining in the sky, we made our way accompanied by family and friends to the airport for our flight to America. Each member of the family seemed to be deeply absorbed in thought as we tearfully said our goodbyes. It was truly a bitter-sweet moment accepting the fact that I was leaving behind my beloved country one more time. Childhood memories, cherished cornerstones of my life, and not to mention some of the best adult years in life flashed across my vision with lightning speed. Were there regrets? Yes, there are a few like having not enough time with my parents before they crossed over to the other side and leaving behind me family and groundbreaking community projects for others to complete. The return back to my roots, the county of my birth, was necessary for it was there that the real me was reclaimed and which has prepared me for what was yet to come.

The flight to America was just as turbulent as the emotions felt by every member of the family. Our eldest son, the teenager at the time, shed tears. His mourning seemed to be for friends, family, and perhaps the privileged lifestyle he was about to leave behind. He had arrived into Guyana from London an inquisitive five-year-old. It took time but he eventually adjusted to the climate, the culture, and the comfort of life in Guyana. Our youngest child, the baby at the time, had a hard time flying for the first time and had to be comforted all the way. We arrived at the bustling John F. Kennedy airport in New

York on a hot Sunday afternoon. The children's attention soon turned to the awe and excitement all around them. Despite hours of careful preparation, we soon discovered that we were not as prepared as we thought. Moving through American Customs and Immigration in New York where we were processed as incoming immigrants went quite smoothly. On the other hand, our best-laid plans for the initial settlement could not have taken into consideration what faith had in store for us. Within twenty-four hours of our arrival, we found ourselves moving through an avalanche of emotions. Unexpected rejection by one side of the family presented a plight that threatened to leave us homeless soon after our arrival. Our only option at that point seemed to be to utilize the return tickets to return back to the homeland the very next day.

While we were still taking in the precarious situation in which we found ourselves, the phone rang ushering in grace and mercy. We were overawed by an unexpected gracious invitation extended to us by another section of the family with help from a total stranger. Loving arms were extended to us and we were taken in by my brother-in-law and his gracious wife into their home. Within the first twenty-four hours of our arrival in America, the first few lines of Sister's prophecy was manifested. This caused me to give attention to the words that followed the accurate prophecy of rejection. When I dropped to my knees in thankfulness to God for making a way where there seemed to be none, Sister's reminder to me of the power of prayer had kicked in.

The morning after our arrival at JFK, the family traveled to Maryland where we were greeted and embraced by loving, welcoming arms. We settled in with in-laws. Life in a new country for us started all over again; only this time, with just what we had managed to fit into six suitcases. We were victims of our government's restrictions on taking US dollars out of the country. Everything we had worked so hard for had to be left behind. In a peculiar way, I was thankful for the busyness of the newly transplanted life which placed the focus on surviving in the present moment rather than on contemplating what had been left behind. It forced me to keep my eyes above the water in a situation where I felt we were sinking fast. I threw myself into the task of getting the children settled into schools. I was learning as much as I could about life in the Greater Washington DC area and particularly, about the American school system. The children came to America with a firm British educational background, well-supported by a Catholic school education in Guyana. Academically, the task of fitting into the school's curriculum was easy for them; social and cultural integration was by far the most difficult. My eldest son, aged sixteen who had just graduated from high school in Guyana, was not at all happy to have to return to school to gain eligibility for his High School Diploma here in America. He became very quiet, withdrawn, and melancholic. When questioned about his withdrawal, his answer gave us food for thought.

"Now I understand that it is not really about race, but rather about being different. In England, I was singled out because of the color of my skin. In Guyana, I was singled out because of my British accent. In America, I'm back to the race card. Wherever you go, Mom, it really is about being different. I can't change who I am." His words struck a deep, dismal chord within me as I had no real way of comforting my child in the midst of his defining moment.

For us adults, finding employment, on the other hand, proved to be a bigger challenge than we expected. We found that we were overly qualified for the jobs typically available to immigrants. With no professional experience in America, resumes had to be rewritten and expectations reexamined and lowered. Much to his horror, my husband found himself living the experience he most dreaded—being an educated *black* man in America with all of its trials and tribulations, and he was resentful. When I left Guyana, I worked at a management level of the country's bauxite industry on loan to the school system to add business education into the High School curriculum. Here in America, being a woman, I was the first to find temporary employment stuffing envelopes at four dollars and ninety-five cents an hour. Believe it or not, I was very thankful. As I saw it, I had at least set my foot on the first rung of the employment ladder. It was a place to start and I was hopeful that it would lead to better employment down the road. In the meantime, my husband's frustration levels ran high with each rejection he received in the job market. He was, however, very persistent—it was one of his best attributes. Three months after our arrival in Maryland, he got a job as a welder. I remember asking him if after working at a management level in the sugar industry in Guyana if he could even remember how to handle a welding torch. His response was,

"We'll see."

The hardships of adjusting to the new school environment, social isolation, and feeling their way around a very different type of family life bonded the children tightly together. Work took me out into the world and opened up opportunities for me to interact with a variety of people. I was slowly beginning to learn firsthand the American way of life. My first real break came when I was hired to work in a large Presbyterian church in Washington DC in the role of a secretary to the Senior Pastor. I'd say that this was the beginning of the next chapter of my spiritual journey. The church library was extensive and beckoned me back to my love of reading. My new boss, a Theologian who had spent most of his career in the field of education, soon became my teacher. He walked me through the four gospels. It was here, on a winter's day, encouraged by the Pastor, that I shared my near-death experience publicly at a noonday lecture at the church for the very first time. I was surprised at how well it was received considering that it was not a well-known topic at that time. The church itself was very much involved in the community. I became a member of a tireless team working with the growing homeless population in the Greater Washington DC area. It proved to be a fitting outlet for the levels of compassion I found rising within me. Going public with my experience brought questions that needed answers and I found myself thumbing through my now-long list of questions in my journals. So it was that on a beautiful, crisp fall day in Washington DC, riding the bus on the District of Columbia's famous Sixteenth street, I spotted The National Spiritual Science Center. Here, I began to spend plenty of my lunch hours researching deeply moving spiritual concepts.

On the one hand, I was immersed in Christian doctrine and community service at my day job at the church. On the other hand, I was reviewing research and learning what it really meant to be a spirit trapped in a physical body. During this unique period of my life, I began to have flashbacks to my near-death experience. The past life information I had gleaned at the record became a recurring theme. It was as if I was being prodded to seek, to look deeper, and to integrate the past life information into my Christian beliefs and way of life. Giving up Christianity was never a consideration in my search. I longed to know the answer to how Christ and Peter walked on water and felt deeply that as Christians, we were nowhere near achieving that feat. The practice of meditation, to which I had been introduced early in my seeking, soon became a natural backdrop to quiet the inquiring mind. "Be still and know that I am God" took on new meaning in my new life of change and struggle. It became a natural, active part of my daily routine in order to keep my sanity. Balancing my findings at the Center while attending lectures there against church doctrine was proving to be challenging. It was in the midst of this unique approach and balance between doctrines that I began to find answers to some of the pressing questions recorded in my journals. It was also where, for the first time in my life even though it had been prophesied, that I began to truly *feel* the strong pull toward the ministry. My boss, the Senior Minister of a historical Washington DC church, also sensed this *call*. He held discussions with my husband to propose me as a candidate for ministry. The request was met with a resounding *no* from my husband. Here in America, I had seen women in the pulpit so my original argument was becoming null and void. However, I found a new way to doubt my suitability as a woman for the ministry. My husband's favorite objection on the subject began to repeat and repeat in my mind.

"Didn't St Paul himself say 'let your women keep silence in church?'"

Life in America was becoming more challenging at the moment.

It was amidst the turmoil taking place in my head that the next piece of disturbing yet life-changing information entered my life and demanded my attention. You could well say that it was a hint at what was to become my life's purpose. Our two sons had become very active in the church community as well as in the field of athletics. My pastor's wife, a middle-aged white woman, invited me to Saturday morning brunch. She had taken the time to welcome our family into the congregation. At the restaurant, I was introduced to Edna. She sang in the choir, a tall, beautiful black, professional woman perhaps a little bit older than I was at the time. While she was polite, she seemed to me to be unapproachable, always preoccupied with her own thoughts.

"Norma, I want you to meet Edna. You two have a lot in common. You both have two lovely sons about the same age who are both athletic."

"So pleased to meet you," was my response.

When our eyes met, I *felt* deep compassion moving from her heart to mine. She paused and sighed as if she was preparing herself to say something awkward.

"My sister, what is it that weighs so heavily in your spirit?" I asked as I prepared myself to listen intently to what she had to say.

Nothing could have prepared me for not only what she said but also the emotion and conviction that accompanied every word that came haltingly and painfully out of her mouth. She looked deep into my eyes as she continued.

"It's about your boys," she said hesitantly.

"My sons? Is there—" She intercepted before I could express the concern that sprang into my mind.

"They are good boys, you raised them well but you need to understand that you are now raising black young men in America. Listen to me very carefully."

"Here in the United States of America, there is something you and your husband need to understand. What I'm about to tell you ain't right, but it's just how it is."

She now had all of my attention.

"And that is?" I was beginning to feel very defensive.

"The talk."

"The talk?" I enquired rather confused.

"If," she continued haltingly then corrected herself, "Not if, but rather when either of your sons gets pulled over by the police . . ."

"Wait a minute, why in the world would you even think that my boys would in any way be involved with the police? My children are well mannered and have been raised to know right from wrong."

"There's a talk."

Now, there was something about the expression on her face that hushed me as I gave her the benefit of my full attention.

"It's a talk that you and your husband must have with both of your boys and it goes like this. When the police pull you over to the side of the road, immediately put both hands on the dashboard and wait for instructions from the officer or officers."

I was all ears. There was an earnestness in her voice that demanded and held my attention.

"Tell them to remain as calm as they can and follow instructions even if those instructions lead to them being handcuffed and taken away in a police car."

"What?"

"The time of arrest is not the place or time for black boys or men to argue for their rights. Let the arguments come from lawyers that you gonna have to hire to defend your boys."

I was appalled at what she had to say. At that time, I had lived in other countries and was never faced with information such as that which came out of her mouth.

Edna got to her feet. She seemed overcome by the effort it took to say what she had to say.

"Take what I just say to you seriously. Your son's lives will depend on it. If you don't believe me, check out the statistics for the number of black boys or men who are in prisons here in America, but better still, who die at the hands of the police. I've been there, worn the tee-shirt, and carry the scars deep in my heart and soul to prove what I am saying to you."

Before I could find the words to express what I was feeling, she picked up her bag and walked away. Later, we became very good friends. She's another one of those earth angels that framed my life. Later, I found out that her son had been one of the statistics she spoke so fiercely about.

Prayer and meditation became the cornerstone of my daily life as a new fear stirred deep within my chest. I found myself asking God for mercy and protection to be bestowed upon my family. I paid keen attention to my children's friends and prayed fervently each time my sons left the home maintaining that prayerful state until their safe return. At the same time, there was a part of me acknowledging the unraveling of the so-called mysteries recorded in my journal. The constant state of prayer and mindful meditation seemed to expand my perception and in a strange way began to raise my level of vibration. As my perception expanded, it felt as if I was doing a dance between the realities of being in the confines of a human body—adapting to life in my adopted country and the rapid unfolding of the spiritual world within. It took the rigor of discipline implanted within me by the elders in my native land—strict adherence to a vegetarian diet, exercise (mostly yoga), and breathwork—the fine art of engaging a holistic lifestyle to keep me grounded and balanced. The inner spiritual world was beginning to open up within me. The way of life that I had been longing, for now, seemed within my grasp. I was indeed fully embracing the challenge given to me by the elders in my native land.

"Strive to walk the talk, my child. Walk the talk."

In 1983, with questions burning fiery hot on my mind, the breakthrough I had been praying for manifested itself. I found myself communicating directly with my spirit guide and the guardian angels assigned to my life. All of nature came alive around me and seeped into me with every breath that I took. I spent a great deal of the free time I did have and weekends walking and relaxing in the park accompanied by my children. It was in the middle of a meditation that I was visited by one of my guides who told me that despite well-practiced birth control by me and my husband, the last of the five children I had requested was seeded into my womb. I was surprised to hear this.

"It's a boy," the spirit guide said enthusiastically.

"His name is Stephen with a 'p' and he will be born on the fourth of July and you need to get yourself to a doctor." It was a bitter-sweet moment for me as we were still struggling to establish independent living in America so there was still a great deal of uncertainly in our lives. As I began to contemplate this and anxiety began to step in, I was given the next bit of instruction:

"Allow yourself to stay calm, dismiss fear from your mind. The pregnancy and delivery would be relatively easy. All is well."

Every one of my other pregnancies had been fraught with difficulty and needed expensive medical intervention. In this case, there was the added burden of having no healthcare benefits. Each time I thought about this supposed problem, a peculiar calm would come over me. Once the pregnancy was confirmed by my doctor, a spiritual revelation followed. I had spent every evening in the week preceding this experience listening to calming classical as well as jazz music. Now I want to share with you, with my son's permission, the answer to a question that occupied my mind from the moment that the pregnancy was confirmed. How does a soul on the other side prepare for entry from the spirit world into this world? I should warn you, however, that language has proven to be very inadequate to describe—the images, thinking, and perceptions of this experience I am about to share. The answer appeared quite unexpectedly.

It was the usual rushed Monday morning. I woke up the kids, packed lunches, got the kids on the school buses, and kept my eyes on the time in order to hop onto the 8:05 am bus that, if traffic allowed, would get me to work just about 9:05 am. Once on the bus, an unexpected wave of tiredness descended upon me. I closed my tired eyes and immediately experienced a slight "shift" at the top of my head—more like a cross-over from one side of the brain to the other. My attention was taken to my breathing. I found myself taking measured breaths as I relaxed and eased my way into the now-familiar meditative state. With the release of the breath, it was as if an entire screen opened up before my closed eyes. My breathing shifted. It became much lighter as I watched with fascination what I somehow *knew* to be the soul of my unborn child in the shape of a swirl of beautiful energetic light that began the task of putting in place the goals and objectives for his incoming life. I found myself captivated by the extraordinary scene outplaying behind my closed eyes. I watched as support personnel was identified for the life ahead (spirit guards, guides, teachers), those who would show the way, as well as family members and friends, were also put in place. A timeline was developed for the entry of each soul that was identified and linked to those who would exit from my son's life using input drawn from his record. This record is the permanent, perpetual, spiritual record that constitutes a library containing all that is, has been, and the possibilities of that which is to come. This was the record I had been drawn to in my near-death experience. Blueprints of planet earth and the surrounding constellations were next consulted. Records of the planet's evolutionary stages and phases were also taken into account. The availability of souls in the spirit world, as well as those whose availability would be needed in the physical world, was established. The timing of all those whose presence and/or input into the incoming soul's development were carefully sculptured into this amazing plan.

The next phase in the process evolving before my very eyes was, believe it or not, packing luggage for the trip. These include knowledge, information, skills, and levels of awareness. It was much like the way we pack here on earth for a trip, except what was being packed were concepts, skills, knowledge, and perceptions—the contents of the luggage for the trip to earth. All of the knowledge from previous lives could not be crammed into the limited space, so decisions had to be made about what to pack and what to store; all done in consultation with spirit guides. In the light of the soul's full spiritual understanding, he made his choices. One-tenth of his knowledge was rendered accessible in the conscious stream of his mind. Nine-tenths of what the soul knew had to be submerged in storage in the subconscious realms of his mind. The economic and wise use of space in the memory banks had to be carefully planned. Some gifts, talents, and knowledge already present within those who were designated as family and friends did not need to be replicated by the incoming soul. Materials for storage was then routed to the subconscious levels to remain submerged during the upcoming lifetime. Think for a moment of yourself or your office downloading computer files for storage; it was the same principle or, for that matter, stacking files you don't need into filing boxes for storage off the premises. The information is retrievable unless of course, you forget where it is stored, and sometimes, we do forget. Some of this information was filtered to an even deeper level of consciousness of what I perceive to be "the supra consciousness level." Material stored at this level, it seemed, would not be retrievable to the soul while on earth. I observed a clause spring into being requiring of him spiritual growth and alignment with universal will and principles in the lifetime ahead. The working material, information, and guidelines for everyday living were then routed to what would become the conscious mind with easy accessibility in order to frame personality.

The subconscious mind was then "flagged" with words, signs, symbols, scent, and rhythmic vibratory patterns peculiar to the individual soul. Icons were implanted which are all active parts of a complex signaling system. With precise timing, the intuitive mind was programmed to release information according to prescheduled timing. With all of this completed, the foundation was set; programming for the trip ahead was established. Timing, it seemed, was extremely important. I perceived that forty days before the soul's arrival on earth, the factors listed here were scheduled to be sorted, tabbed, labeled, and sealed in place in the consciousness levels. The stage was set; the signposts of the lifetime were firmly established. As I continued to observe with keen interest the entire system, which now resembled the blueprint of an architectural drawing, I was exposed to waves of radiant, iridescent light and somehow knew that the debugging of the created file was taking place. Radiant dots of light implanted icons here and there into the completed plan. These were visible to me in the form of globules of light. Spiritual support staff gathered to beam signals of light and love into the system. The whole process was breathtakingly beautiful. There was so much love being projected that it reminded me of my own cross over from the darkness of the tunnel into the brilliance of light and love. I opened my eyes with a jerk to find myself stretched out on the back seat of the bus. Paramedics were all around me ready to transport me to the hospital. They had experienced a great deal of trouble waking me up but once I fully awoke, I felt energized with all of my processing capabilities intact. At the time of writing this book, my son is about to graduate from college with a bright and fulfilling future ahead of him. I have had the privilege to observe those implanted flags rising on the horizon that are his earth life. With the ability to see the lines, geometric symbols, and light in his aura, I look upon my son with amazement as he moves through the trials and stages of his life. He is living out the rhythmic patterns brought about by the challenges and changes written into his life pattern. He is reminded often to be gentle with himself for I have been a witness to the care with which he chose and set the conditions for this lifetime. His smile reminds me that it is all worthwhile.

The process described here has been an eye-opener and a blessing for me but I cannot say with any certainty that it is the way in which all souls have been prepared for entry into this world. Perhaps, who knows, this profound experience in 1983 set me up to acknowledge the depth and "sacredness" of life. The process helped me to fully appreciate why they had sent me back from my near-death experience with the words "there is indeed more to life than meets the eye." It certainly shifted my perspective from despair to our world to one of positivity and hope eternal. Could there be a universal plan that supports the needs of each individual soul? That possibility of a concept seemed very real during the review of my own record. It gave me the hope and the courage to engage and fulfill the work that emerged as my life's purpose. Much later, during another mind-blowing meditation, I observed that my son's soul remained conscious of all that it knew until the moment of its birth into the world where the entire system was sealed and became the hard disc of his life. The prophecy of a smooth delivery was indeed fulfilled. It took thirty-two minutes of labor; the smoothest delivery anyone could ask for and my son was ushered into the world. Soon after the birth of my son, yet another earth angel showed up quite unexpectedly in my life.

We were desperate to find suitable and responsible daycare for my newborn baby. On our meager salary/budget, we could not afford the cost of reliable daycare for a newborn baby. With all of my previous children, I did not return to work until they were enrolled in kindergarten. The thought of leaving my baby to be cared for by strangers while I returned to work brought on feelings of guilt and tugged heavily at my heartstrings. My spiritual guide assured me that help was on its way. A young woman who needed a mother figure in her life, having lost her own mother at an early age and whom I befriended in Guyana, offered to travel to the USA, live with us, and take care of my son. She entered into the family, fitted in extremely well, and so had born and nurtured a friendship that has been an example not only to my own children but to others who have also been blessed to observe it. Penny came to live with us and soon became a functioning part of our family life. She found a night job so that I worked by day and she by night. To this day, my son considers himself to have been raised by two mothers. God has not blessed Penny with children but on Mother's day, she receives flowers and blessings much as I do from my son for her part in helping to raise him. Her presence in our midst strengthened the bonds of family here in America. There was a very special agreement between us that she would also honor the family's motto on the importance of education. I was also aware that her father's desire for his daughter was also for a good education. She honored both of our wishes and thereby created an example for the young children in my family and blessed us both when she graduated here in America with a Masters of Science degree in Human Resource Administration.

The search for a way to consciously return to the light and uncover my life's purpose burned brightly in my spirit after the birth of my son. It was a passion that was hard to explain. I began to feel a pressing urge to study and to better understand energy and vibration. It was an intensity that was not easy to explain. Then, the strangest thing happened. I responded to a knock on my front door to find a petite nun standing there. I invited her in. We exchanged names and she came, she said, because someone had given her my name and telephone number on one piece of paper and my address on another. She had lost the first piece of information and took a chance on knocking on my door. The nun had what she thought was a dilemma. She had fallen in love with one of the priests in her order and was bewildered about what to do about it.

As she settled comfortably in my favorite chair, she sighed, shook her shoulders, and closed her eyes. She began to outline her problem and in midsentence, she stopped, cleared her throat, and the next voice I heard out of her was that of an Irish male.

"Good day, I have a message for you. Will you receive it?"

I was shocked and surprised myself when I heard myself responding in a rather shaky voice.

"Yes, I will," I responded calmly despite my racing heart.

"You will very shortly be asked to attend a conference in London. You must accept the invitation and attend. It is very important that you do."

"Sorry, but financially, I could not possibly afford to do something as expensive as that."

"Lack of finances is not your problem right now. Your problem is an expired passport and you cannot travel on an expired passport." My mouth literally fell open and he continued:

"Everything else is in perfect order."

"But you don't understand," I stammered.

"It is very important that you attend this one. Thank you for accepting the message, take care of the problem, and have a blessed day."

The nun sitting in the chair opened her eyes, took one look at my bewildered face, and said:

"Are you all right? What happened?"

"You brought me a message from an Irish gentleman that told me my passport was expired and I'd need to travel."

"What did you just say?" She asked in a trembling voice.

So I repeated the statement as calmly as I could.

Pulling open the drawer in the nearby china cabinet, I reached for my passport, opened it up, and gazed in disbelief. My passport was indeed expired.

"What does it say?"

"It's expired all right."

The nun in the chair, an expression of total disbelief on her face reached for the small pouch she had placed on the floor beside her, got up, and literally ran out of my house. I picked up the telephone as if in a dream and watched myself dial the Guyana Embassy's number. Arrangements were then made to have my passport renewed with a degree of urgency. Having done my part, I waited patiently for further developments.

The waiting was not for long nor was it in vain. Just a few days later, a young lady for whom I had provided life coaching services turned up at my house to invite my participation at an upcoming Energy Conference in London, England. I was absolutely flabbergasted at the speed with which the series of events occurred. When I graciously declined the invitation, she asked why. I responded that in all honesty, I did not have the finances to attend the conference. Another one of those earth angels stepped in and offered the use of her American Express card to cover all of my expenses. In return, she wanted me to bring back a detailed report of the conference, its materials, and its speakers. I arrived in London on a Friday evening tired and fatigued from my trip. It was the opening night of the five-day conference. The scheduled keynote speaker was Dr. Valerie Hunt. I was not at all familiar with her name or her work. The introduction, however, took my breath away. She took my spiritual understanding to the next level with these opening words:

"Twenty-first-century medicine is about guided information systems and light."

It felt as if I was struck by a thunderbolt of light. There was intensity, purpose, and a call to action in that statement. I perceived shock waves of light filling the room and I was instantly re-energized.

At the end of her mesmerizing speech, I joined the line to have the book I had bought autographed. As I inched up closer to the top of the line, she looked up and pointing directly at me, said:

"You are the one who got me out of my laboratory."

"Me?" I responded weakly with a question mark resounding in my voice. "I've never seen you before in my life," I retorted.

"Very few people can get me out of my lab, but you did. I have a message for you." Needless to say, I attended every session, class, and/ or lecture she was involved in at the conference. On the morning of her departure, she summoned me down into the lobby and gave me her message and these parting words.

"Your gift is for you to transfer everything in your brain into the brains of others."

"But that is impossible," I protested, "My father always said . . ."

"For others, it may be impossible, but for you, it is what you came here to do, and remember: Twenty-first-century medicine is all about guided information systems and light."

And then she got into her waiting taxi and was gone. I returned to the United States and compiled a detailed report about the conference, then I read everything I could get my hands on that was written by Valerie Hunt and began to receive insights from the realms of spirit around the concepts of light refraction, the brain, and higher consciousness.

With every new insight flowing into my consciousness, I was being urged to seek out the clearing and cleansing of body, mind, soul, and spirit. Just as I was contemplating how to do this in-depth cleansing, there entered into my life another pair of earth angels quite by accident. I got off the train at the end of the ride at Gaithersburg Metro station in Maryland. My attention was drawn to a young Native American couple squatting on a grassy knoll. As I walked past, the female among the two smiled at me. I returned the smile and she asked:

"Do you live around here?"

"Yes, I do. Do you?"

"No, we're here to do a sweat lodge," the male responded smiling.

I had never heard of a sweat lodge but I was strangely aware that this was the answer to the longing of my spirit for deep cleansing.

"What is a sweat lodge? What is the purpose?" I was keenly interested in the answer to my questions.

"You're invited to attend. It's tomorrow. Come find out for yourself."

"Really, you're inviting me?"

"We'll be right here on this spot tomorrow at eleven a.m. If you're interested, show up and we'll take you there. We'll wait for an hour just in case you are late but at noon, we must leave for the ceremony."

"That's very generous of you. I'll have to think about it."

"Don't think too hard. If you show up, we'll be on our way together. If you don't, that's okay too."

My children nearly had a fit when I shared the experience and announced that I intended to take my new found friends up on their offer. My daughter's response was:

"You mean your new acquaintances. You're not seriously thinking of doing this?"

"Every part of my being is crying out to do this and I will."

So it was that on a Sunday morning I journeyed with two of the sweetest, kindest people I had the joy of knowing and participated with my native American brothers and sisters for the first time in a sweat lodge. Praying and sweating in a sweat lodge may not be for everyone. For me, I sweated out pain, regrets, negativity, grief, and loss. We honored each other in that lodge. I sweated, cried out to my God, felt loved, and emerged lighter when I left. It was to become a yearly cleansing activity for me for the next five years of my life. This experience taught me a lot about the healing concept of "release and renewal" and I went on to develop the technique. I was beginning to feel ready for a visit back to the light. The study of new information downloaded into my spirit by night reinforced by meditation, mindfulness, and visualization was preparing me for the journey and back to this world's reality However, I had no real way of knowing how, when, where, or if it would ever take place. My guides were peculiarly silent on the subject. I did sense that I was being led along yet another pathway to living out the biblical term "You cannot put new wine into old skins." Release of old belief systems, habits, and practices in that sweat lodge opened up doorways to yet another level of my spiritual journey with new, clear lenses through which to sense and feel the journey back to the light.

In the midst of what seemed to me to be reordering of my senses, a question asked of me during my near-death experience began to repeat itself in my mind.

"What have you done with your life?" followed by yet another pressing question.

"What is your intention for the rest of your life?"

I found myself answering that question aloud in the middle of one of my meditations.

"To make my way consciously back to the light and back," was my response.

The response was instantly coded into my consciousness.

"First you must consider your purpose: the reason why you were sent back and its place in your life."

There was now a haunting feeling within me that I had been shown my life's purpose during my near-death experience. I found myself struggling to recall the memory. This internal struggle brought a great deal of processing into my head as well as a yearning in my spirit. I longed for the guidance and reassurance of my spiritual teachers who were now oceans away. It was time to use the tools of prayer and meditative silence before God that they had given me. Introspection brought me face to face with an acknowledgment of the many compartments of my life—family and children, career, social responsibilities, and the most pressing issue on my mind, my marriage.

The question asked of me at the record during my near-death experience "What have you done with your life?" began to replay in my mind. I could *feel its relevance* at this important time of my life. As a couple, we were two heads living in two different worlds; we'd grown miles apart. He, having fathered two children outside of the marriage; me now walking with a new, very strong spiritual perspective, seeking divine guidance. I opened my eyes from a particularly calm and serene meditation early one morning to the memory of a moving scroll of female faces crossing my consciousness during the meditation. These faces represented the number of women my husband had been involved with during the course of our marriage. Among them were familiar faces of friends and acquaintances. In a strangely calm and serene state of mind, I finally acknowledged that we had in fact been living separate lives under the same roof for a long time. It was the recognition that my twenty-three-year marriage had in fact ended and the realization that I had chosen to live in denial for a long time. It was in that same state of calm and serenity that I initiated a separation discussion with my husband. One year after our separation with legal complications looming and the need for adequate health coverage for the children, I started divorce proceedings. Financially, I was broke; supporting five children and trying desperately to keep my head above water was not easy. Once again, almost on cue, the next earth angel appeared on the threshold of my life. A rather prominent Jewish lawyer heard of my plight and after interviewing me, provided legal services to me on a pro bono basis.

CHAPTER TEN

Adjusting to life as a single mother with only one paycheck meant I had to learn new money management skills. Wearing and balancing the variety of hats needed to keep the family halfway stable took some serious adjustments. My belief and faith in the knowledge that there was a divine plan for my life kept me going. My five children, ages ranging from eighteen to two, found themselves struggling to respond to a major change in their lives. They were right there beside me responding to the adjustments of their lives being subject to being raised by a single parent in difficult times. While I assured them that we would come out of the impoverished state in which we found ourselves, I was not at all sure when or even how. So, I let my mind go back to my childhood, to the days when I would hear my father, the teacher, repeat over and over again what has now become our family's motto: "Education is the key that will get us out of poverty." This reminder took me to a series of patterns in my life—memories from my life in London and how education became the key to our family's prosperity. So began the mindfulness process of keeping myself and the children true to the family's motto. I wrote those words on every single piece of paper I could get my hands on and kept it visible all around the house while I dropped to my knees before Almighty God with the words from the hymn:

> What shall I do?
> What steps should I take?
> What moves should I make
> Tell me Lord what shall I do?
> I'm going to wait for an answer from you.
> I have nothing to lose, tell me Lord what shall I do?

In an effort to increase my take-home pay, I found myself changing two jobs within three months and picking up a part-time job along the way. Managing all the pieces of functioning as a single parent and keeping family together meant juggling far too many hats which all proved to be painfully demanding. As in most divorces, family and friends either took sides or felt too awkward to continue friendships/relationships. Isolation began to border onto depression and I found myself praying to God to keep me from falling by the wayside. Penny, though much younger than I was, became a tower of strength as we clung together in our support for the children. Music by now was becoming a big part of my daily routine; it helped to preserve my sanity. I could see behind my closed eyelids the beautiful moving colors and rhythm of the musical notes. Soon, I was able to discern pieces of music that helped to calm my fears—the ones that strengthened my resolve and the ones that kept my creativity flourishing. Along with the sheer pleasure of listening to music, I was beginning to appreciate one of its major roles on the planet— ushering in change. In the meditative state, I soon discovered that it was possible to channel streams of light from musical patterns into people, places, and things. I sought out and read everything I could get my hands on in relation to the connection between sound/ music, rhythm, matter, and the brain. Although at the time I did not identify it as such, I was beginning to open up to energy and sound healing.

The excitement of this new discovery guided me to practice the art of focus. When I did, I found that I could direct streams of light into the chakras (the seven spiritual centers located in the physical body). I practiced on the people around me including my children and soon discovered that my focus could and had improved their moods. While caught up in the discovery and magical experience of sound, I was given my very first solo assignment by my guides to establish my very first spiritual "Circle" here in America. A specific time was set aside each month where truth-seekers gathered to engage in the work of developing practical spirituality. Images of the very site where the circle would take place were given to me from the spirit realm. In a dream, I found myself being chauffeured in a limousine traveling along a very rocky country lane. On both sides of the lane, there were beautiful, huge oak trees completely dripping with green moss.

". . . and this will be the site of your first 'Circle,'" the male voice in my dream announced. I awoke first amused by the image of a luxurious chauffeur-driven limousine traveling down a rocky country lane, and secondly, I was given this arduous task with only one sketchy detail to go on.

At the time, I knew next to nothing about the landscape of the American countryside. I certainly did not have the financial stability to put up the seed money to begin such an ambitious project. Soon after this revelation, the next earth angel came into my life with perfect timing and very relevant information. I was introduced to a cartographer, a gentleman who hailed from New York, who was quite knowledgeable about historic sites and mapping. He quickly identified the area in my dream as Penn Center in Beaufort, South Carolina. This information allowed for the commencement of planning using a team of three volunteers. The next set of instructions was given the same way as the first. It provided the ethnicity of the prospective attendees who turned out to be seven African Americans, one African from the motherland, four participants from the Caribbean, one Hispanic, and one Caucasian. Responses to our advertisement produced exactly the numbers and ethnicity that was given to me in the dream state. With the revelation in place, I arrived at the airport the day before the rest of the party. Due to a miscommunication, there was no one there to meet me. When I called the center, they arranged at short notice for a limousine that had taken a newly married couple to the airport to transport me on the return trip to Beaufort. Thus, I found myself arriving in fine style traveling along a country lane with majestic moss-draped oak trees on both sides of the lane just the way it had been shown to me in my dream. It was a lesson in understanding that there is an element of universal planning at work in all of our lives at all times. The rest of the party arrived the following day.

There was a distinct air of excitement when the group gathered together for the introductory session. We sat in a circle and honored the ancestors who had initially occupied this space. We worked through a series of release and renewal techniques. The rest of the week was spent in sacred silence, in communion with nature, and going within. Since then, a total of ten "circles" has been initiated with the blessing and energy of this original group. Included in the ten are circles established overseas. One in Jamaica; on my very first trip there, I fell in love with the people, the island, and the beauty of the ocean. A circle was established there and I have returned to Jamaica many more times taking retreats with groups of people who were interested in the pursuit of practical spirituality. Mexico was the next adventure on the list where me and my youngest daughter were welcomed with so much love and genuine hospitality that I was truly humbled by the experience. It was yet another opportunity to initiate and leave behind us a circle.

An unexpected invitation to visit Japan extended to me by Shinji Shumeki of America to participate in a three-day "vigil of peace" changed my life phenomenally. It afforded me five precious days in Japan to meet and greet with its people and to learn more about the precious value of light and its healing qualities. Set in the mountains close to Kyoto, Shumei's Founder's Hall was a masterful piece of architecture seating well over fourteen thousand people. It was truly an impressive sight to behold. Its interior resonated with light, love, peace, and an amazing mix of people from all over the world. I learned firsthand from my hosts by way of exposure and experience. Their hospitality and eagerness to spread love, light, and cultural diversity throughout the world were extremely moving. It was a five-day journey of walking the talk that reminded me so much of the simplicity but intensity of my former teachers. The experience reinforced my appreciation of the purity of energy and the raising of vibrations to take humanity into higher levels of consciousness. Until this blissful experience in the mountains, these words were good intellectual concepts. By the time I left Japan, the cherry blossoms and bonsai gardens, the "living sacredness" of the mountains, the people, and above all the role of art in raising and awakening inner consciousness became fully integrated into my being. My mother often used words that fitted in very well with my experience of the Japanese culture: "Who feels it, knows it Lord." Another "circle" was initiated and left behind in Japan.

Upon my return to Maryland, I felt a real affiliation to mountain tops and a sense that somehow, a serious work had been brought to the threshold of my consciousness, and I was right. My insight and "knowing" seemed to have been expanded and brought recall of memory from my near-death experience in relation to my purpose. In the dream state, I saw myself walking in light into the darkness of prison. The light inscription on the wall of the prison read: *"Set the captives free."* I awoke from the dream with a vivid memory and the face of a white male who, I was reminded, was designated to conduct my ordination. In seeking enlightenment of the meaning and interpretation of the dream, I was instructed that it was time for ordination, an absolute necessity, to give me the authority to reclaim lives. At that time, there was no name to the face I had been given and therefore, I was at a loss to know where to begin. As it turned out, I stopped one Saturday morning to pick up a magazine to read while I waited for my son's basketball practice to end. When I pulled up at the magazine rack, there was the magazine with the picture I had been carrying all those years on the cover. It was the face and the story of Rev. Dan Chesboro who had recently felt that his life's purpose was to "call" the priests of Melchizedec back into service. I threw myself into reading and consuming everything I could get my hands on about the order and made contact with Rev. Chesboro. At the time of contact, he was in England. As soon as he returned to the States, we began discussions and arrangements for my ordination. After years of doubt and questioning my suitability for the ministry, a strange, beautiful calm came over me and I *knew* deep inside of me that this was indeed part of my destiny. The ordination took place on a mountain top in Virginia. It was for me deeply "sacred," bringing yet another level of awareness of the sacredness of service and an abiding calm and stillness. My love for mountain tops has since increased and every year, I make the journey to the mountain top to spend quiet, meditative time atop of the Blue Ridge mountains either here in Virginia, in America, or in the Blue Ridge mountains in Jamaica. Each trip has provided me with strength, guidance, and courage to submit to Almighty God's will for my life's purpose on earth.

The "calling" to enter into prisons to provide service was beginning to sit very heavily in my spirit. The opportunity presented itself when the church that the family attended got involved in a Christmas holiday activity to bring cheer to the children in the Washington Children's Center. I was excited to learn about this program designed to take art supplies into the center to allow the children to make holiday greeting cards for their parents and/or guardians. This seemed like the perfect opportunity since I had a fear of guns and handcuffs. Somehow, I expected that these would not be present in a Children's Detention Center. Training and orientation for the team were done at the church and we were all excited to experience our introduction to the children and staff at the center. Upon arrival, the first thing that struck me was the dismal and gloomy appearance and atmosphere of the building housing children. When we entered, the protocol and the search of our personal property was another turnoff. Everywhere, there were guards with handcuffs attached to their belts. Once we entered the facility, the sound of iron bars in the form of gateways clanked shut behind us was a fearful experience for me. Finally, we were escorted into a large room that doubled as a dining room as well as the room where the children received family, visitors, and volunteers.

CHAPTER ELEVEN

Time moved swiftly bringing new experiences and change with perfect timing. My children moved from high school and college graduations to delightful wedding ceremonies adding love, new faces, new cultures, and new life to the family. I was blessed to gain son and daughters-in-law who all fit well with the family structure. In the meantime, two new pieces of music found a way into my life. These were both given to me as thank you's by two young people, one male and the other female for the healing that had taken place in their consciousness by way of life coaching. Stephen, a Hispanic young man, entered my home one day, excitedly taking the steps two at a time to arrive in my presence.

"Norma, look what I found," he said excitedly waving a CD in his hand.

"Who is it, son?" I asked feeling the excitement of the moment.

"It's Miles, but I don't think you heard this version of *Time After Time*. As soon as I heard it, I knew this one was for you."

"Really? Why do you think so?" I asked pushing him to explan to me what it was about this particular version of the music that spoke to him of me.

"I can't explain it. Just listen." He placed the CD into the player and hit the play button. I was immediately drawn to the unique orchestration behind Miles's trumpet. I closed my eyes and found myself magically traveling through globules of beautiful light. No amount of the world's currency could have provided the joy and bliss I felt in that moment. Later in my spiritual journey of service, this particular piece of music became instrumental in transforming many addictive lives. It became the perfect information system that was needed in the appropriate circumstances to be guided by the light of the light bearer. The second piece was a surprise birthday gift from my blond female, a daughter from another mother. She took me to a George Winston concert at Washington DC's Kennedy Center. When those beautiful chords from the Pachelbel's *Cannon* rose in the Kennedy Center, I floated out of my body and experienced my spirit as light as a feather roaming somewhere at the top of the White Hills of Dover situated in Kent, England. In my travels, while living in England, I yearned for the opportunity to see the Hills and to somehow find my way to experience the view from the top. Yes, the universe does grant unto us the desires of our hearts when we take the time to clear the clutter within in order to prepare for the blessing.

Just around this time in my life, the "calling" to enter into prisons to provide service was beginning to sit very heavily in my spirit. The opportunity presented itself when the church that our family attended got involved in a Christmas holiday activity to bring cheer to the children in the Washington Children's Detention Center. I was excited to learn about this program designed to take art supplies into the center to allow the children to make holiday greeting cards for their parents and/or guardians. This seemed like the perfect opportunity since I had a fear of guns and handcuffs. Somehow, I expected that these would not be present in a Children's Detention Center. Training and orientation for the our team was conducted at the church. We were all excited to meet the children and staff at the center. Upon arrival, the first thing that struck me was the dismal and gloomy appearance and atmosphere of the building housing children. When we entered, the designated protocol for the search of our personal property was another turnoff. All around us, there were guards with handcuffs attached to their belts. An eerie feeling came over me, I *sensed* that the guards were really there to physically enforce discipline by any and all means necessary. Once we entered the facility, the sound of iron bars in the form of gateways clanking shut behind us was unnerving. Finally, we got to the children and I was visibly shaking.

Nothing prepared me for the emotion of pity and remorse that erupted inside of me to see children incarcerated. It took everything I had to stop myself from throwing up right there and then. I was a mother who could not handle the conditions under which these children were held. As soon as we entered the room with the children, they all scurried to claim an adult mentor. A thirteen-year-old boy clung to me raising the most pitiful eyes to me with the words:

"Will you be my mentor?"

"That's why I am here," was my response.

"You will come back, won't you?" he pleaded with his eyes locked into mine.

"Yeah, yes, I'll come back."

"Cause you know most people don't come back."

We spent no more than twenty minutes on that first visit and received instructions on the rules governing our visit. Then, the visit ended with the children being first escorted out of our presence as Ryan, my assignee, kept his eyes focused on me until he was out of the room. When we left, I walked to the car and threw up. I got into that car and had a talk with God.

"I can't do this, I am not strong enough for this. I am a mother. I cannot bear to see children living in confinement," I was pleading to be released from my commitment.

All that week, I wrestled with my conscience and each time, I convinced myself that someone else may be better suited to handle the conditions than I could. However, I could not get Ryan's stricken face out of my mind. So, I determined that I would go in one last time to face Ryan and tell him that I could not be his friend. I skipped week two agonizing over my dilemma. Feeling very badly about my decision, I braced myself and showed up at week three. As soon as the volunteers entered the room, Ryan sprang into action, ran over to me, grabbed my hand, and looking deeply into my eyes, said excitedly:

"You came back. Thank you, I'm so glad you came back."

I did not have the heart to look him in the eyes and deliver my carefully rehearsed speech. So I swallowed hard and saw the project through to the end but did not sign up for the next round.

My life slipped back into its usual routine. However, I could not shake the feeling that my life's purpose had something to do with prisons. The subject became a matter of distraction during my meditation sessions keeping me from experiencing complete relaxation. So, I thought perhaps working with women, mothers of these children might be better. I began filling out application forms to become a volunteer to work with women in prison. Lack of response was causing me even more stress and frustration. I started to share ideas and concepts with friends and acquaintances who were social workers. My calls into the prison system continued to be met with silence; messages left on answering machines never yielded a return call. I was just plain frustrated. In the meantime, through the guidance of spirit and automatic writing, I began to receive and put together a psycho/spiritual approach for the relieve of trauma. So, in the meditative state, I asked for guidance on where and how this process would be most useful.

Among the many concepts that I have had the privilege to learn on my spiritual journey is that earth angels are real, they are encased in an earthly body, and that they are always seeking and embracing opportunities to be of service on the planet. The very next earth angel came along, entered my life, and brought phenomenal change. She brought to life this proverbial African saying: *"hand wash make hand come clean."* Her name was Betty and we collaborated together to make one of her dreams come tru—a week-end retreat and follow up intervention for homeless women. So, it's an early Saturday morning; I had just finished my morning devotions and meditation when the phone rang. It was my friend Betty, the social worker. By this time, we had become close friends.

"Norma," she said, "I have a dilemma. I'm coordinating Howard University's annual conference on Substance Abuse Intervention Strategies and today's keynote speaker just called me to say his mother just died and he is on his way to the Carolinas."

"So sorry to hear that. That's a big problem but I don't know of anyone I can recommend."

"I was hoping you could fill the spot."

"Why? How?"

"Your concepts of intervention are, well, unique."

"Oh no, I am not a psychologist, a certified counselor, or an expert on the subject."

"But Norma, you have an engaging voice and a unique, integrative approach to intervention."

"Not feeling it, girlfriend."

"Norma, let me finish. You are here, where would I find someone at such short notice?"

"Keep looking, I'll be over there. Now if you don't find someone else, I guess I'll try it." So I show up at Howard University around noon to find a very affluent speaker on the stage, well prepared, and extremely knowledgeable on the subject with all the right visual aids. I was elated.

"Betty, I'm so glad you found a speaker. He is great," I said with a sigh of relief.

"He has another appointment and has to leave in ten minutes, then you're on."

"Are you kidding me? Who in the world will listen to me after listening to your expert?"

"Norma, you're my luncheon speaker. You will be just fine," she said.

"You're kidding, right? Do you know how hard it is to hold the interest of a lunch crowd?" At that point, the presentation on the stage came to an end and the crowd burst into a rapture of applause. My heart sank as the speaker exited the stage. I went right over to congratulate him on his presentation.

"That was excellent. I learned quite a few things today, but I can't follow that."

"You will do just fine."

"No, I won't. I wouldn't listen to me after such a fine presentation."

"I tell you what, I've got to be somewhere, but I'll stay for the first few minutes of your presentation. I'll be right here. You'll do just fine. I want to hear your ideas on the subject."

I took to the stage inwardly shaking like a leaf. My outer demeanor, I was convinced was being managed by my spiritual guides, it portrayed an outer calm I did not feel on the inside. I opened my mouth and gave an outline of the psycho/spiritual approach that had been given to me from the spirit world. It highlights the power of music/rhythm to lift the spirit, break down trauma, and restore self-confidence. He stayed for the entire talk. When I walked off the stage, he approached me with these words:

"When you are not speaking doing this, what do you do for a living?"

I heard the strange-worded response coming out of my mouth:

"Never mind what I do for a living, I'd like to have the opportunity to test the concept I just outlined in prisons."

His response stunned me.

"Wednesday, noon, D.C Jail, staff entrance, I'll be there. Be there."

I was astonished, I could not believe that just like that in the middle of doubt, a door had just been opened.

So was born the beginnings of my work in prisons starting as a volunteer and working in that capacity for fourteen years. It was undeniably my gateway to fulfilling the purpose of my life. The writing I had seen on the wall "set the captives free" was beginning to manifest itself into action in my life and it was exciting but also overpowering. My journey began on that Wednesday at noon when I was formally introduced and inducted into a male "circle" by a renowned psychologist at the facility in Washington DC. Up until then, everything I had been taught led me to believe that it was inappropriate for a female to lead a male circle. Later, I was to discover that spiritual leadership has more to do with levels of vibration and consciousness than it is about gender. The awakening from my near-death experience, the challenges of my life, and the spiritual road I had traveled seemed to have equipped me with both. Acceptance into the circle put me to work with a dynamic treatment team of committed professionals—clinicians, administrators, and community leaders—a diverse group of people whose mission was to pilot a project to bring treatment into prisons, operationalize change, lower recidivism, and implement a sustainable re-entry process for ex-offenders. I was assigned along with other volunteers to work alongside professionals, clinical staff driven to provide services in an eighteen-month pilot program. My specific task was to integrate spirituality into the clinical model. With the high levels of enthusiasm all around me, I soon began to feel comfortable and at ease ready to throw myself into learning as much as I could of the environment. Somehow, God or the universe found a way to erase the fear of the guns and handcuffs all around me. Entering and leaving the institution, the rules, regulations, and search protocol did require mental adjustment on my part. When irritations came, I reminded myself that it was all in the interest of safety and my new found purpose kept me going.

My close-knit family which consisted of my own children, other children whose lives had been affected by my intervention, and friends expressed reservations about a female working with male felons in a volunteer capacity. These doubts and concerns initiated a family meeting to express these concerns and to address the fears for burn-out. I acknowledged that their concerns were valid and reminded them of the power of God's mercy. There was so much to learn in that prison environment. We all gave a lot, but I personally also received more than I could possibly have given. The stages, phases, and adversities of life were there to be read like an open book. The potential for change, rehabilitation, and redemption was also ever-present in everything that we did. The respect and confidence the clients displayed often moved me to tears. There was one quotation that kept me grounded throughout the twenty-seven years of service. It was a line from one of Bob Marley's popular songs:

"The biggest man you ever did see was once a baby:"

Despite the information contained in inmates' records, I chose to see and relate to each participant as a divine soul birth into the body of a baby. Figuring out how, when, where, and why that body and mind got turned on to criminality was the job of the staff psychologists. As part of a team of dedicated experts, I was mindful to stay in my lane of bringing my modest gesture of hope, grace, and spiritual transformational techniques to the table. Illiteracy and poor reading and processing skills among the inmates proved to be a challenge in the creation of learning materials. The number of inmates struggling with anger, trauma, and drug addiction was high. It was as much a learning curve for me in this new environment as it was for the clients in the program. My spiritual process sought to lift the spirit, raise vibrations, and bring hope into traumatized lives. In the intervention process, responsibility, healing, and redemption became strong watchwords among the residents as well as the staff. Well-orchestrated music/rhythm in the form of music therapy became the backdrop to intervention. Bob Marley's words "You running and you running and you running away but you can't run away from yourself." These words and the accompanying melody became the backdrop for serious self-discovery. Much of what was taught to me by my spiritual teachers were shared with the inmates in my circle. Sunday morning Bible study and worship services were established in the institution with voluntary participation of the Christian as well as Muslim inmates.

Requests began to pour in from two other prisons asking me to speak and requesting collaboration and program development. A women's program was soon established in Delaware that brought intervention and re-entry services to a women's facility. I resigned my day job as the director of an inter-faith housing coalition to accept a Federal government contract to provide spiritual and intervention services to inmates in a newly established state-of-the-art re-entry center in Washington DC.

I was now also traveling twice a week to volunteer my services at a Delaware Maximum Facility. The staff there were keenly interested in introducing the psycho/spiritual technique as their intervention process. While there, I discovered that Sunday worship was lacking due to the absence of a prison chaplain. I volunteered to provide the service on a weekday and proceeded to do so. Unknown to me, someone had been passing information on my sermon topics to an inmate on a death row. So quite unexpectedly, I received a request to provide counseling services in my capacity as a pastor to an inmate on a death row. He had lost his final appeal and was heading to execution. There was concern in my mind about the appropriateness of this request and of my ability to perform the right kind of services for such an inmate. I sat in the stillness of meditation and asked for guidance, then took the request to my spiritual teacher at the time, which resulted in rather interesting dialogue.

"I have to admit that the thought terrifies me." I was being absolutely honest.

"I do sense fear in your aura. Is it your own emotions that you fear, or is it the stark reality, the finality of death row that scares you?"

"A little bit of both," was my response.

"I don't know if I have what it takes to . . . I don't know," shaking my head.

"Have you prayed and meditated on this request?"

"Yes, I have and out of my meditation, I can now hear the words—'set the captive free.'"

My teacher got to her feet and started pacing, and there was what seemed like a long period of silence. When she lowered herself gently into a chair, she reached out and tilted my chin so she looked at me directly in the eyes. Her voice soft, almost a whisper as she said:

"You are just being asked to show up."

"But . . ." I protested

"Let's look at what we know so far. You have asked with consistency and shown me your purpose. We know from your listening to the inner voice that this purpose you seek involves prisons and therefore, prisoners as well. You stilled yourself in meditation, asked, and was given the words 'set the captives free.'"

"You traveled so far, true?" Our eyes locked; hers with compassion, mine anguish.

"You can't stop now, I know what I'm feeling right now?" I was too scared to ask what she was feeling.

"You're about to know what God's love really is. You sensed it on the other side." Suddenly, I was shaking; there was so much conflict present within me. One side of me wanted to scream out to the universe the resistance I felt within. The other dominant part of me refused to let the sound out. My teacher wrapped her arms around me in a tight embrace. When we broke the embrace, she whispered ever so softly into my ears:

"Norma, God is asking you to show up. Just show up."

Acknowledging that last whisper as a divine answer to the pressing questions on my mind, I decided and announced my intention to move forward with an initial visit. After a particularly intense meeting with the warden and staff at the prison and tedious paperwork, permission was granted for my visit to death row. My family was informed of the decision and it was clear that they were anxious and concerned. My son speaking on behalf of the entire family said:

"Mom, you've always let your faith in God be your guide, do what you are called to do." On the morning of the scheduled visit, I left Maryland early. Driving to the backdrop of beautiful piano music helped to calm my nerves. Accompanied by two armed security guards, one on each side of me, we began what seemed like an endless journey along corridors and doors that led to death row. There was no exchange of words between us. Here and there, the silence was punctuated by the sound of iron doors clanging shut and heavy footsteps. The inmate's name was Jerry Watson. I had deliberately refrained from reading his record or transcripts of his trial. What I did know was that he was sentenced to be executed and had lost the last of three appeals; also, the fact that he had specifically requested my services of spiritual support was humbling.

Finally, we arrived at our destination. My accompanying guards held a wall of silence throughout their observation. Behind the bars of the cell in front of me stood a black male, hands clinging to the bars of his cell as if his very life depended upon it. I sensed his eyes taking in every aspect of the scene playing out around him. Our eyes met. I could not quite place my finger on the peculiar range of emotions all around me.

"Hello," I said in the best positive voice I could muster up, "I am the reverend you requested."

"Hi," he responded calmly, "and thank you for responding to my request."

"You are most welcome," I responded trying to be as gracious as I could.

"First, I wanna apologize for what they put you through to get up here. It's how things work around here." His tone was truly apologetic.

"No worries, how are you doing?"

"Best I can under the circumstances. Thank you for asking."

The time allotted for the visit was controlled so I went straight to the fundamentals of what I considered to be the process.

"I'd like to start off by letting you know that I am not here to judge you, defend the system, or for that matter, push religion upon you. I'm here to listen, and if I can, provide what spiritual guidance I have to offer."

"I appreciate that."

His tone was that of relief. It was much better than when I first entered.

"So, tell me what is it that you expect or for that matter, require of me."

His eyes met mine and for the first time since I entered, I saw stark, raw, naked fear in those eyes. At the moment, it scared the hell out of me. Questions I was prepared to handle or erasing intense levels of fear was something I was not at all sure I was capable of doing.

"What's the difference between religion and that word you use—spiritual? I got questions"—lifting the Bible in his right hand—"questions from what I been readin' in this book."

"This word, this thing y'all call redemption. Is it real?"

"Well, there's food for thought. Three places to start. Do you have an objection to prayer?"

He bowed his head and closed his eyes. We prayed and just like that, the first session I was dreading on death row ended. Escorted back to the entrance of the prison, I got into my car, let out a big sigh of relief, and then experienced a flashback to the fear I saw in his eyes. In the long journey back home, I convinced myself that Jerry needed a much more experienced spiritual advisor. He needed someone like a retired prison chaplain. I right there and then dedicated myself to find and bring him one. On my second visit, I excitedly told him about the retired, experienced spiritual coach I had found and recommended that Mr. Watson put himself under the advisement of this individual. His response was very pointed and quite clear:

"I can see you got drama around this. Can't say I understand. You preach stuff but now you looking to chicken out of the real deal." In his eyes, I could see raging anger.

"I prayed on this, did my research, and the 'spirit' led me to you. If you can't do it, I'll do my Bible by myself, alone. I don't need your damn preacher man. Thank you very much."

Leaving the prison, I felt numb and kept hearing my teacher's voice repeating in the form of a whisper in my ears.

"Just show up."

Well, I did, and I did not like what I saw, and the feeling of being vulnerable was somewhat overbearing. With those thoughts racing through my mind, there came an additional set of words:

"And . . . God will do the rest."

The atmosphere of my third visit was a lot lighter. I turned up with a recorded version of the Bible to speed up reading and discussion. Mr. Watson on his part presented me with a list of questions he had created from his personal reading of the Bible as well as the Quran. His second most probing question was:

"Who in the Bible said, 'Ask and it shall be given unto you?'"

"Those were the words of Christ," I responded confidently.

"Who was he speaking to at the time?"

"His disciples, why?"

"That's my point exactly. He was talking to men who dropped everything and followed him. They all had rights. Me, guilty of many, many of sins—could that apply to someone like me?"

I left the session with that question burning like a torch in my mind and made the decision to take it into my meditation session. This took us to discussions on redemption.

We went on to work on the use of simple self-discovery and transformational techniques that he could do during the week. An interesting, respectful, but beautiful connection emerged between teacher and student that demonstrated the basic human need for human communication and connection. Years of solitary confinement on death row awaiting the results of two appeals had instituted a routine of discipline into my student's life. He was respectful at all times and his gratitude began to shine through in his mannerisms.

We worked on scriptures that had to do with the concepts of forgiveness, repentance, redemption, resurrection, and the afterlife. I shared my near-death experience. The student became quite outgoing and even excited about his progress. He began to verbally acknowledge the release of fears and even identified the onset of spiritual growth. However, on this particular day, I showed up to find him unusually quiet and deeply introspective. We sat each one of us on their side of the bars in respectful silence for quite a while. Then he said quite somberly:

"You know this ain't no card game."

"I'm sorry," I said apologetically, "I don't know much about the rules of card games."

"You know there ain't no hope of winning here." Desperation was present in his voice.

The implication of this statement screamed at me, but I forced myself to remain silent. Turning to face me after what seemed like a long pause, he said in a now-controlled voice:

"Do you know, you're the only person I'd turn my back to without looking over my shoulder." Here he paused, looked me directly in the eyes, and said:

"I trust you."

"Come on, Mr. Watson, you did have a life before all this . . . childhood—"

"I never trusted anybody, no one, even when I was a child."

After that comment, I'm at a loss for words. So I fidget, held his gaze, but remained silent.

"Release me, Rev.," he said with emphasis.

He looked at me directly in the eyes, and in a childlike whisper, he repeated the request. By now, I cannot mask my surprise. I understood in my spirit that this was not an idle request but rather a spiritual one. So, I attempted to enter a sense of humor into the moment in order to regain some level of composure.

"Tall order . . . if I ruled the world of justice . . . maybe . . ."

"I mean, release my soul." I looked into his eyes and I could see that he was serious.

"Close your eyes." He relaxed and dutifully closed his eyes.

I began to hum the words of an old negro spiritual hymn.

"Yes, we will gather at the river,

the beautiful, the beautiful river.

Gather with the saints at the river that flows by the throne of God."

My death row student closed his eyes and drifted away into the meditative state he had been practicing for a while. We had talked about meditation. I had provided reading materials on the subject. This was, however, the first time I had used my voice to take him there. I found myself guiding him through the darkness of the tunnel where I had traveled during my own near-death experience, held him at the exit of the tunnel so that he could behold and absorb the intensity of the crystal clear white light on the other side, and guided him back into the physical with the chant of a psalm. When he opened his eyes, there was a smile on his calm, peaceful face. I was amazed at how simple and easy it had been to take him to the light.

"Do you know the song *Déjà vu*?"

"Yes, as a matter of fact, those lyrics haunted me there for a while, why?"

He smiled; there was no need for further words or discussion of the experience.

"Now," I said, putting a level of briskness and authority into my voice.

"Let's get back to where we were—the second scripture on redemption."

"No need," he said with a corresponding lightness in his voice.

"I got it." A beautiful smile crossed his face.

There was no doubt in my mind that my student had travelled out-of-body. His awareness during the meditation had taken him to a near-death-experience moment. In his own words, he indicated that he no longer feared what was before him. At the beginning of our journey together, he had tried hard to convince himself that he would experience his execution as a mere injection that would send him into the unknown. What he had confided to me then was that he was not afraid of death but was terrified of the fire, hell, and damnation that he had absorbed from his childhood religious experiences in church.

"Now I *know* that there is light beyond the darkness and light is love and love is God."

I knew in that moment that my task of facilitating the release of fear was over.

The night before the execution, I had paced in silent prayer and meditation, consulted, and prayed with a group of clergy who was supporting my efforts from outside of the facility. On execution day, I arrived at the prison and was escorted by a posse of guards and prison staff into a small room, a circular table, and two chairs positioned in the center. My heart was racing, unsure of how my emotions would stand up to the day's events. The inmate was brought into the room with shackled hands and feet escorted by armed guards. We sat facing each other as armed guards positioned outside of the door. This was a part of his right to receive one-on-one spiritual counseling allowing him the "rite of confession" before his execution. With a beautiful, relaxed smile on his face, he greeted me:

"Rev," he said, "celebrate with me. In a few hours, I will be with my God in the light."

His excitement was contagious. He took a seat across from me and continued by sharing flashes of his life that were really funny. He reminded me of people in his family life and asked me to convey his last greeting to them. We laughed together at some of the ironic moments of his life. Then, there was a very somber moment.

"You never asked, but I want you to know anyway. I've been guilty of a lot of shit in my life that I ain't proud of but I ain't never kill nobody, Rev. It's okay though. I'm tired of the fight and I'm ready to go home."

"I am so grateful for the gift of redemption; you took me to my *awakening.*"

"God's will, my son. I'm only blessed to be the vessel."

"Now, the last wish of a dying man. After this session is over, I want you to leave the building. I don't want you witnessing my execution, walking the earth with that image."

"But I have—" He raised his eyebrows, forcing me to stop in mid-sentence.

"An image is worth a million words, right? So, so hard to erase right? You taught me that. I want you to remember Jerry Watson in the peacefulness of this room. We gonna say a short prayer." Then turning his eyes heavenward, he said:

"Thy will be done on earth as it is in heaven. Amen"

"They gonna take my life. They'll take me to the left, spectators will go to the right. But you'll go straight ahead and out of this building."

Flashing pearly white teeth, he smiled and reminded me of something I had taught him.

"I want you to treasure the images of this hour—the grace and mercy of God brought to me by your very presence in the last days of my life. Bless you."

"Thank you, I don't really know what to say."

"You've said it all. You're the one through which God spoke to me."

By this time, I was trying hard not to show any emotions for the moment.

"Give thanks and praises," he said glancing up to heaven.

"My request is my gift to you. It is my birthright as a man to protect women. You thought I wasn't listening, huh! I heard and will take with me every word you have said to me. They'll take my life today, but they can't take away my birthright. I still have something to give while I got the 'sacred' breath within me."

"But . . ."

"Shh. Walk with the memory of these last moments," he said smiling.

The knock on the door indicated that the session was over and the guards came rushing in to take him away. We never said goodbye, Mr. Jerry Wilson and I. Rather, they got him to his feet heavily chained at the hands and feet to be taken away to prepare him for his execution.

"See you around." He lifts his shackled hands as if to wave.

I fight back the river of tears rushing into my eyes. I wave as the tears come gushing out against my will. Despite my desire to be present at the execution, I honor my student's wishes.

Later in the parking lot, *the bell tolled*. It signaled to the community that the execution of Jerry Wilson had been completed. However, it signified to me that the soul of Jerry Watson was released from the prison of a traumatized body/life into the loving, luminous light I had come to know so well. With eyes lifted to heaven, a smile crossed my lips and I offered thanks for Jerry's release remembering the joy of my own crossover and how I emerged from that dark tunnel into the light.

In a discussion a few days later with my teacher, she asked me a question I was only too happy to answer.

"Have you learned the lesson?" she asked looking deeply into my eyes.

"Yes," I said with a smile, "God asks us to show up so his mercy can shine through."

"Congratulations!" she said, "You have now earned the coveted title of 'wisdom keeper' on the planet."

THE END

CPSIA information can be obtained
at www.ICGtesting.com
Printed in the USA
LVHW041258260723
753241LV00010B/819